PLAY SMART AND WIN

How to Beat Today's Most Popular Casino Games

VICTOR H. ROYER

A FIRESIDE BOOK
Published by Simon & Schuster
NEW YORK   LONDON   TORONTO   SYDNEY   TOKYO   SINGAPORE

FIRESIDE
Rockefeller Center
1230 Avenue of the Americas
New York, New York 10020

FIRESIDE and colophon are registered trademarks
of Simon & Schuster Inc.

Designed by Stanley S. Drate/Folio Graphics Co. Inc.
Manufactured in the United States of America

10   9   8   7   6   5   4   3   2   1

Library of Congress Cataloging in Publication data

Royer, Victor H.
    Casino magazine's play smart and win : how to beat today's
most popular casino games / Victor H. Royer.
      p.   cm.
    "A Fireside book."
    1. Gambling. 2. Games. I. Casino magazine. II. Title.
III. Title: Play smart and win.
GV1301.R65   1994
795—dc20   94-3973
                                            CIP

ISBN: 0-671-88024-1

This book is dedicated to my dear mother,
Georgina S. Royer
with love and respect for the incredible
achievements she has made in her life.

Contents

Acknowledgments

"No man is an island" may be an old cliché, but there is deep truth in these words. In a global sense, as human beings all of our lives are interconnected in some way. On a more personal level, all of us have a group of people, friends and business associates, whose own lives have a profound effect on who we are, how we live our lives and what we can achieve.

A famous man once said: "If I can call one man my friend then I am richer than all the Kings in history." In this way I am fortunate indeed to be so wealthy.

Among those who have touched my life are many special people, all of whom have contributed in one way or another to this book. This is an opportunity for me to thank them, and to acknowledge direct contributions by many of them.

I wish to thank my mother, Georgina S. Royer, for her tireless dedication and a lifetime of sacrifice and effort that provided me with the opportunity to realize my ambitions. This remarkable lady has never faltered in her consistent and considerable support of all my endeavors, and throughout all the trials of our lives has remained a solid rock of talent and resources [which cannot be bought]. All the words I could ever write wouldn't begin to tell the incredible story of her life, or the value of what she achieved and made possible for me.

My friend Tom Caldwell has been a veritable fortress of support to me. He helped alter my life, recognized the value of my goals, and consistently helped to foster them on a daily basis. His knowledge and experience in the gaming industry have been a helpful resource to me, and the hundreds of hours we have spent together discussing gaming have also helped me to crystallize my thoughts. Tom has also contributed by reviewing this book as it was being written and has provided many valuable comments and suggestions.

I would also like to thank Denny Weddle for providing me with my first opportunity in the gaming industry in Las Vegas. Denny was instrumental in introducing me to Tom Caldwell, and it was Denny who first opened the door to me at Weddle/Caldwell Advertising and Marketing Agency in Las Vegas.

I also extend my thanks to Ned Barnett and his wife, Karen Ann Barnett, for their assistance. As my literary agent at the time it was Ned who found a way to get this book published.

To Nick Viorst, my editor at Simon & Schuster in New York, I extend my gratitude for his support and appreciation of this book. For any author an understanding editor is worth his weight in gold.

Tim Illies, a remarkably talented gaming executive in Las Vegas, has been my good friend for many years. His knowledge and talents in gaming have provided me with an insight into the business of gaming that I could not have hoped to gain so quickly otherwise.

I would also like to thank Sergio Lalli, who gave me my first assignment as a gaming writer in Las Vegas when he was editor of the *Nevada Casino Journal*. Sergio is a noted author in his own right, and his encouragement and support I greatly value.

I offer my appreciation to Catherine Jaeger, managing editor of *Casino* Magazine, who is an extremely bright and talented lady. Cathy has provided me with encouragement and a continuing opportunity to publish my views on gaming. She has become a valued friend, a respected source of professional opinion, and a darned good editor.

To these people, and those whose names appear in a special section at the end of this book, I give my sincere thanks.

Foreword

When Victor Royer first approached me about writing features for *Casino* Magazine, my impression of him was: a Las Vegan with a talent for writing and an abundance of entertaining tales to share. That's a good combination of qualities to have in a feature writer, so we struck a deal.

On numerous occasions he calls to discuss story ideas, and our conversations invariably end up with his recollections of amusing stories and with my being in stitches as I became privy to the humorous frailties and idiosyncrasies of some of the most famous people to ever hit the "Strip" in Las Vegas. The people in my office are often left wondering who could elicit such a response from the managing editor.

After getting to know Victor and learning more about his zealous pursuit of the Las Vegas experience, it became clear to me that he is a man who seriously studies people and events. That's why his accounts of them are so entertaining. He picks up on the finer points and pays close attention to detail. I later came to the conclusion that Victor approaches everything that way.

There's no question that being involved with a gaming magazine has its perks, not the least of which is that people who are located in gambling centers frequently invite you to visit them. Victor was no different. He often said I should come to Las Vegas and let him show me the area from his perspective. He knows that city as only an insider could, he said. He knows what machines to play and how to win at every game offered in Vegas, he said. You can imagine my reaction: "Sure, Victor. That's what everyone from Las Vegas says." "Yes, but I'm writing a book about how to win," he countered.

Well, during my second visit to the City of Lights, I finally had the opportunity to meet Victor. And of course, I let him show me around. His knowledge of the city is indeed plentiful and valuable. Not until we visited the casinos to try our luck, however, did I realize his true expertise. Victor advised me about which machines to play, which payouts to look for, and, in some instances, which machine manufacturer to look for with certain games. I was astounded. Once again, he was sharing the benefits of paying attention to detail.

The blackjack tables were another aspect of my learning experience. Playing to win may not always be the most fun, but it has its monetary rewards.

As Victor stood behind and advised me about when to hit and when to stay, I kept track of the times I would have made different moves and lost my bets. I would have played like any other visitor. After all, one sort of expects to lose money and chalk it up to entertainment. That thinking has no place in Victor's world, though. He insisted that I play smart. I did. And I won.

We toured other games and he quoted probabilities, but then he explained to me in layman's terms what they meant to my bankroll. I came away from this experience knowing that Victor is a full-fledged gambling expert. What an advantage I had over the House with his advice! I made the most of it.

Victor is one of the few who can play smart and win. Fortunately, he is willing to share his knowledge with those of us who usually don't play as smart as we could and, consequently, lose. With Victor's book you too can avoid the pitfalls of gambling and come away with the richness of experience that I had the pleasure of receiving firsthand from Victor himself.

Catherine Jaeger
Managing Editor
Casino Magazine

Preface

A man walks into the Riviera in Las Vegas, buys two dollars' worth of nickels, walks over to a three-coin, three-reel, three-line video slot machine, and begins to play. Six pulls later he collects $50,000. Not bad for an investment of ninety cents!

This is a true story. I saw it happen. At the time, it seemed incredible that someone could have this much luck. So I began to pay more attention to the people who gambled, how they did it, when they played, what they played, and how much they played.

I soon discovered that the man who won the $50,000 wasn't alone. There are many others like him, and, for the most part, they all seem to have one thing in common: Yes, they are very lucky, but there is something else . . . they are smart players, and they win. It is through observing people like this that I came to appreciate how much more often such smart gamblers win than those who arrive in town with wide open eyes and an empty brain . . . soon to be accompanied by their empty wallets.

During the course of several years, I have discovered there are many levels of gambling knowledge and competence. At the top would be those relatively few who can truly be considered "professional" gamblers. These people exist, but their lives are not the glamorous ones we think of. There's no "James Bond" atmosphere to such professionalism. It is a hard job and a deadly tedious grind vested with pitfalls, dangers, and uncertainty.

At the other end are those who enjoy games of chance for the fun of it, with little expectation of winning something. These are the casual gamblers, the vacationing gamblers. They represent the majority of the population. Perhaps you are one of them. If you enjoy gambling, or have never tried it but would like to, or simply don't know as much about it as you would like to, this book is written for you.

Play Smart and Win is *about* gambling. What you will *not* find here are complex charts, tables of mathematical calculations, betting systems, and so on. What you *will* find is a great deal of easy-to-understand, easy-to-remember basic information on gambling, designed to make you a smarter, better player all around.

This book presents an overview of games that are offered in the modern casino; it explains how to tell the good slot machines from the bad ones; demystifies the "payoff" schedules; recounts numerous entertaining and informative stories about successful gambling; and, most of all, provides some very specific advice to help you play "smarter."

There are many books on the market that will teach you how to play any gambling game, from beginner to pro. The purpose of *Play Smart and Win* is not just to give you this knowledge but to provide it in a straightforward manner and to show you how to *apply* that knowledge. Although *Play Smart and Win* does explain the fundamentals of gambling games, the focus of these explanations is not to embroil you in detailed analysis of game theories but to provide you with sufficient knowledge to allow you to make better decisions—decisions about which games to play, which machines to play, and how to play them wisely.

If you've never been to a casino—or even if you are a regular visitor—you can help yourself play smarter and better just by keeping your eyes and ears open, and knowing what to look for.

Introduction

Gaming is no longer the sole property of that once lonely town in the middle of the Nevada desert, Las Vegas. Gaming is fast becoming a nationwide phenomenon. New casinos are springing up in the Midwest, as well as on Indian reservations throughout the country. More and more people are patronizing casinos, cruise lines, Bahamas resorts, the many local Bingo and lottery games, as well as the glittering casinos of Nevada and New Jersey. And the more people that come, the more money the casinos make. But all this money-making need not be one-sided. Like no other form of entertainment, gaming offers the customer an opportunity to also make money . . . by winning!

In the 1980s, when "yuppiedom" was so popular, my friend Mac was the perfect yuppie. He made great money and visited Las Vegas every chance he could get. Just as frequently he would come back and brag about how much he lost. I finally got tired of listening to him and asked why he lost so often. He said: "Because the games can't be beat." So I asked him why he keeps going. And he said: "Because there's always a chance I *will* win!"

Mac is pretty typical. Like him, most gamblers lose. Indeed, very few people do win. There are many reasons for this, but the main one is that the vast majority of people, just like my friend Mac, go to casinos knowing little or nothing about the games they will encounter. They may know how to play *some* games. Maybe they even think they know how to play them well. But a great majority of all of today's casino players don't have a clue as to why some games are structured better than others, why some slot machines and Video Poker machines pay better than others [even though they look *exactly* the same] or why they lose instead of win.

Players lose primarily because the odds highly favor the casino. These odds are "security percentages" that the "House" (the casino owners) factor into the games to assure themselves of a profit (called the casino's "win") and also to safeguard themselves against one too many lucky streaks from some wise gambler.

Yet the games *can* be beaten. One way is the professional way: Become a student of the game, learn to count cards, have a large bankroll, lots of time and guts, and grind out small profits over a very long period of time. This is possible. But professional gambling is extremely tedious and the average vacationing gambler hasn't the time, patience, or inclination for it.

The other way to beat the games is to be lucky. I was at the Mirage when it opened at Thanksgiving 1989. On that day one unassuming gentleman visited the casino, quietly bought some brand-new shining Mirage silver dollars, sat down in front of the Megabucks machine, and began to play. Six pulls later an amazed crowd watched as four Megabucks symbols lined up on the bottom line and this smart and lucky player collected $5.6 million dollars!!

This man was very lucky. But that does not mean that he was not also a very smart gambler. After all, luck simply means being at the right place at the right time, and it can be helped along. I've done it, and thousands of other gamblers have also done it. Helping Lady Luck along is neither as surreal as it sounds nor as impossible. Most smart gamblers know that when a new casino opens, the best event that the owners can hope for is a big winner who will receive national publicity, or at least a lot of smaller winners who will all add to the excitement of the opening day. This is the kind of free publicity advertising money can't buy. The man at the Mirage on opening day knew it.

It all boils down to what to play, when, and how. Your "luck" comes into play with your power of choice. Remember that word—choice! It is a *very* important word for any gambler.

"Choice" is important because it is the only weapon the gambler has that he can use time and time again against the House. Remember, the House—the casino owners—have already built into the games their profit potential. For you to overcome that profit potential and maximize *your own* profit potential, you must employ your own edge: choice.

Luck and choice are a marriage of profit and convenience, a partnership for winning; but choice is the major instrument of winning for the gambler. However, to be able to make the correct choices all gamblers require at least some knowledge—knowledge of the games, how to play, and, even more important, how to apply that knowledge to the available gaming options. In all games, in all betting situations, in everything associated with gaming, the choices you make directly determine what the House will or will not get from you.

When you enter a casino you are suddenly faced with a multitude of choices: many varieties of video games, slot machines, table and other games. So many options are enough to quickly overwhelm the senses.

The fact that there are so many different table games and variations on games, so many different slot machines and variations on slot machines, so many different video poker machines and variations on them, and so many lights, buzzers, bells, dings, signs, graphics, colors, and more lights is *not* an accident.

The entire atmosphere of a modern casino is *specifically designed* to confuse and disorient gamblers. Even if you visit a casino once a month, which most vacationers don't do, you are nevertheless subject to this sensory overload to a point where your mind goes into overdrive. Reason is overcome by adrenaline and the "I must try everything" personality suddenly appears even in the most rational and normally sensible human beings. And the first thing that vanishes with this mental state is your ability to make good choices.

That is why the casinos are designed the way they are—not to rob you of money, but to minimize your powers of choice. Casinos don't have to cheat; they'll make huge profits anyway from the millions of gamblers who get caught up in this sensory overload—people to whom money suddenly means nothing and the desire to win just as quickly gives way to an urge simply to play.

Once you have decided to gamble, these myriad choices await you: Which game will you choose? How will you play it? How much to bet? When? What slots to play? How are they different? When to play them? Should you try two coins, one coin, three coins, five coins? Quarters, dollars, five dollars? Blackjack, Poker, Craps, Roulette, Baccarat, one deck, two decks, four-deck shoe, six-deck shoe, eight-deck shoe? What limits? One hand or two or three? And so on, and on and on and on and on!

Get the picture? Choice means a lot. No wonder the casino owners want to make sure you lose the sense of it.

I'm not trying to give the casinos a bad rap. After all, they provide the entertainment. By gambling there you are paying for this entertainment. Casinos are in the business of providing an adult playground, and a lot of us like it. That's why we go there in such great numbers year after year. But we don't have to be dumb about it. Anyone who says, "I'm going to the casino to lose my money" is just plain foolish. Everyone who goes to gamble should go there with winning in mind, or at least not with losing in mind. The fact that most lose is indisputable. But some *do* win, and a few win *big*.

To win big is often just the result of blind luck, which is different from the kind of smart luck I've been talking about. On New Year's Day 1990, actor Charlie Sheen walked out of Cafe Roma at Caesars Palace in Las Vegas with 3 dollars in change, put it in a slot machine on his way out, and won $7,777.00! The same thing happened to a nice old lady from Minnesota who had seventy-five cents in change and won over half a million dollars in the same manner. And to the man who bought $2 in quarters to pass the time while waiting for his wife . . . and hit the same machine for $555,000! That's blind luck!

This book isn't about blind luck. It is about another kind of luck, the kind of luck you make for yourself. This book is meant to help the novice or vacationing gambler make better choices, make those vacation dollars go a little further, and perhaps win some money in the process. Blind luck can win you the super jackpots, the multimillion-dollar bonanzas you hear about in the news. This is the kind of luck that wins the lottery. But the luck your choices can create helps you win more regularly.

In order to make the better choices, or at least to know that you *have* choices and *why* you have them, some knowledge of the games and their differences is very important.

What, for instance, is the difference between 6/5, 8/5, and 9/6 Video Poker machines? And why do they exist? What do these differences do? And what is the difference between a two-coin, three-reel slot machine and a three-coin, four-reel slot machine? This is all very valuable information. And what is the difference between a single-deck Blackjack game with a full table of seven players and the same game one-on-one with the dealer? A two-deck game? A six-deck shoe? These are some of the items of knowledge discussed in the following pages that will help you make better choices.

Each chapter in this book selects a game and outlines some of the most basic items of knowledge that are very helpful in making good choices. In each chapter I also briefly discuss how to play such games and how to apply some of this knowledge to good gaming choices. Gambling can be a profitable form of entertainment; when you go to a movie, you pay your money at the box office, see the movie, and your money is gone. But when you go to a casino and gamble with that money, you also have a chance to win *more* money! That's the big difference in this form of entertainment. But entertainment it is, and entertainment it should stay. It is for fun, not for food. It is my hope that this book will offer you an instructive, informative guide to casino gambling. This will make your visit to the casino not only more enjoyable, but, very likely, more profitable.

1
VIDEO POKER

There are many different varieties of Video Poker machines currently available in major casinos, and all of them are based on a singularly simple premise: the Five Card Draw poker game. If you have ever played Poker you already know the fundamentals. And even if you are not familiar with Poker, its simple rules make Video Poker one of the most entertaining games to play and by far the most popular of all modern computerized slot machines.

To understand how Video Poker came to be so popular—for the player as well as the casino—it is necessary to look back briefly over the gaming industry's recent history.

Today's casinos are far different from the casinos of yesteryear. As recently as twenty years ago, casinos consisted primarily of table games. Slot machines were looked on merely as diversions for the wives and girlfriends of the gaming patrons, and slot players in general were looked upon as incidental customers. Casinos tolerated them, "real" gamblers looked down upon them, and the consensus among casino bosses was they were a necessary nuisance.

Those were the "good old days" of casinos: the era of the high-roller Craps player, the Poker master, and the Blackjack aficionado; the era when dinner shows still included dinner, and when entertainment meant comfort in the booth, sipping champagne and relaxing at the expense of the resort.

But in the 1970s two major events brought an end to this heyday of the casino business. The first was a recession triggered by the 1973 Arab oil embargo, which, coupled with inflation and a severe credit crunch, abruptly halted the flow of easy money that Las Vegas, and the gaming industry in general, had taken for granted since the days of "Bugsy" Siegel in the late 1940s. The second, and certainly more far-reaching development, was an FBI probe into Mob control of Las Vegas casinos, resulting in allegations and investigations, IRS audits, arrests and trials. This effectively wiped out Mob control, and gaming changed forever.

But the indirect result of this crackdown was that even those operators and casino owners considered unaffiliated with the Mob suffered. Suddenly government investigators suspected everyone. Allegations flew thick and fast, and the public began to stay away. Many well-established casinos went broke, and others teetered near collapse.

It was the all-time low of the casino business, the bleakest period in the glorious history of Las Vegas. But it also proved to be a turning point for the gaming industry. During this time, in the late 1970s, the future of Las Vegas, and gaming in general, hung in the balance. Las Vegas could have become a ghost town, and gaming could have disappeared altogether. Fortunately, it did not happen. Today, Las Vegas is at the forefront of gaming, and the gaming industry as a whole is perhaps the top recreational industry in America.

This was primarily the result of two factors: the application of the computer chip to gaming, and the birth of corporate ownership of casino resorts. When the Mob left town, the existing casinos were acquired by corporations and enterprising individuals who, backed by public and private moneys, invested in the casinos because they saw a profitable future. However, before the profit came, there were growing pains.

As with most corporate takeovers, the first thing that happened was that the old operators were replaced by an avalanche of lawyers and accountants. The direct and immediate benefit of this to gaming was that these professionals were very quickly able to satisfy the FBI and IRS that the gaming business had been cleaned up.

But in the process, during daily reviews of financial operations, these people reached some startling conclusions—and none was more startling than the remarkable imbalance they discovered between casino profits from table games and those from slot machines. The accountants crunched numbers and quickly found that casinos made as much as 80 percent of their profits from slot machines, and only 20 percent from table games—quite a stunning conclusion at the time. Suddenly the lowly slot player became very important.

It was around that time that an enterprising gaming inventor came up with the idea of using poker, the grand old American card game, as the basis for a computerized slot machine. Almost overnight the Video Poker phenomenon was born. The concept and the program were remarkably simple. Little did anyone know at the time just how revolutionary they were.

In order to recover quickly, the casino industry had to do two things: first, attract players in great numbers; and, second, make large profits fast. Both needs were perfectly served by the Video Poker machine (and, shortly thereafter, by computerized slot machines).

By introducing Video Poker, the casinos could immediately offer something new, simple, entertaining . . . something *everyone* could play without feeling intimidated by the old casino gamblers and owners. And, likewise, the casinos could immediately begin to rake in the quite sizable profits generated by players of these new machines.

The effect was immediate, though at first not all of the change was for good. Table games were pulled. Lounges and restaurants were closed. Stages were torn down. Floor space was expanded and filled to capacity by endless rows of machines. Soon casinos appeared more like video arcades than casinos. And then the novelty began to wear off. It was time for the lawyers and number crunchers to move on and make way for the new breed of casino operator.

Gaming entrepreneurs like Bill Boyd, Chuck Ruthe, Steve Wynn, Jack Binion, Don Laughlin, Jeanne Hood, Conrad Hilton, Jackie Gaughan, Kirk Kerkorian, Bob Stupak, Bill Bennett, Mel Larson, and many others became, and still are, the premier personalities of the new Las Vegas. They took the reins and transformed a dying industry into the giant it is today. These men and women and others like them quickly appreciated that video parlors alone wouldn't suffice.

The modern gambler demands variety, diversity, entertainment, grand style, fantasy . . . all the stuff that dreams are made of, and all the stuff the myth of Las Vegas is made of. To re-create this atmosphere and cater to the majority of new gaming patrons, themed hotel resorts were built. Equally important, all casino areas were well supplied with an ingenious balance of Video Poker, slots, and table games. The package was completed with the trappings of luxury, which ranged from the tasteful to the gaudy. But all of these changes were well thought out, both independently and collectively, among the new breed of owner-operators. These are the casinos you see today.

And it all began with the Video Poker machine.

♦| HOW TO PLAY VIDEO POKER |♦

Video Poker is probably the simplest interactive gambling game now available. It is an interactive game because you can choose which cards you will keep and which cards you will throw away in the draw. Its simplicity lies in the easy-to-understand rules of the Five Card Draw poker game. I will therefore begin with a short explanation of

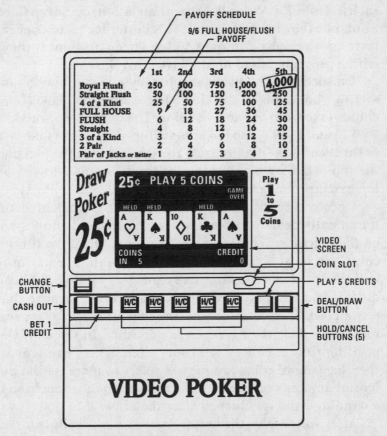

	1st	2nd	3rd	4th	5th
Royal Flush	250	500	750	1,000	4,000
Straight Flush	50	100	150	200	250
4 of a Kind	25	50	75	100	125
FULL HOUSE	9	18	27	36	45
FLUSH	6	12	18	24	30
Straight	4	8	12	16	20
3 of a Kind	3	6	9	12	15
2 Pair	2	4	6	8	10
Pair of Jacks or Better	1	2	3	4	5

A standard Draw Poker 9/6 Video Poker Machine.

Five Card Draw and then expand on how this applies to Video Poker.

In the Five Card Draw poker game you are first dealt five cards. You then have the choice of keeping any or all of them or throwing away any or all of them. For each card you throw away, you get another to replace it. The object is to improve your "hand" (the final set of five cards you decide to keep) and make it into a winning hand. This is the format currently used as the basis for the computer program that runs virtually all Video Poker machines. There are other Video Poker machines now being introduced, such as Hold-Em Video Poker and variations on Seven Card Stud, but they are so few that it is better for us to concentrate on the most common Video Poker machines, those with a program based on the Five Card Draw.

On such a Video Poker machine, you begin play by inserting your coins in the slot. Almost all Video Poker machines take from one to five coins. The only exceptions are $5, $25 and $100 Video Poker machines, which can take two or three coins as "maximum." You can *only* win the jackpot, the top prize, by playing the maximum coins allowed on the machine you are playing.

Once you deposit the maximum coins, the machine automatically deals you the first five cards, displaying them on the machine's screen. If you play fewer than maximum coins, you must hit a lit button labeled "deal." The machine will then deal you the same five cards you would have been dealt if you had played the maximum coins, because that set of cards is determined by the machine's program immediately after the first coin is deposited in the slot. Depositing more coins will not alter these five cards; therefore, more coins are played solely to increase the potential amounts of money to be paid out by the machine if a winning hand is achieved after the draw.

After you receive the first five cards, a row of buttons on the machine lights up, usually with the word "hold" written on each one. These buttons are used to keep the cards you wish to hold. There are five hold buttons, one for each of the five cards you have been dealt.

Normally, the hold buttons are directly underneath each card, making it easy to see which cards you are selecting. When you press any one of the hold buttons, the word "held" will appear above or below the corresponding card. This means that you have chosen to retain the card as part of your hand, and when you take the next step in playing this hand, the machine will keep the card on the screen. In effect, *you* have chosen to keep the card. Pushing the button simply tells the machine what your decision is.

You can hold any one, two, three, four, or all five cards, as you wish. Once you have selected the cards you wish to hold, you must press the deal button to continue the hand. The machine then keeps the cards you selected and throws away the rest, immediately dealing you replacement cards for the ones you didn't hold. If the combination makes a winning hand, the machine pays you automatically and the hand is over. Most modern machines pay on "credits," with the number of credits you have won typically displayed either at the bottom right-hand corner or the top left-hand corner of the video screen. For instance, if your win is five coins, the machine will indicate the win by displaying the word "winner" and running up the amount of five coins on the "credit meter."

After the credits are paid, the words "player paid 5" will usually appear on the screen, and this message will stay displayed until the next hand is played. Of course, if you win thirty coins, this message will say "player paid 30," and so on. You can then play the next hand by using your credits. Simply press the "bet" button, once for one coin, twice for two coins, and so on; or you can touch the "play maximum coins" button, in which case the machine will automatically deduct five credits, the normal maximum bet for most machines, and automatically deal the next game. The whole process is then repeated over and over each time you press this "play credits" button until your credits are gone, or until you decide to collect them.

With the credit-meter option, the machine will pay the amount of your win to the credit meter each time you win. Each time you lose, the credits you used to play with are gone, lost in the same way your coins would have been lost on a losing hand if you had inserted coins in the slot. If you have credits left on the credit meter and wish to collect them, you can do so at any time after the current hand is completed simply by pressing the button marked "collect." The machine will pay you by dropping your coins in the tray mounted below the machine.

◆| PAYOFF SCHEDULES |◆

Although there are many different kinds of standard Video Poker machines now available, all such machines—except those employing "wild cards"—offer the same "payoff schedule." The payoff schedule refers to the hierarchy of winning hands and tells the amounts that these winning hands will pay you if you hit them.

Payoff schedules on the majority of Video Poker machines employ the same hierarchy, which reflects the value of Poker hands as determined by the rules of regular Poker. On most Video Poker machines, the lowest hand that gives a payoff is "jacks or better," which pays even money—in other words, for a pair of jacks, queens, kings or aces, this hand will pay you five coins for a five-coin bet: even money.

The payoff schedule, from best to least as it appears on the machine's payoff display, is as follows:

ROYAL FLUSH   A-K-Q-J-10 in any sequence, but all in the same suit: spades, clubs, diamonds, or hearts.

STRAIGHT FLUSH	Any straight in any sequence, all in the same suit—e.g., 6-7-8-9-10.
FOUR OF A KIND	Any four of the same value card—e.g., 5-5-5-5.
FULL HOUSE	Any three same value cards with any two same value cards—e.g., 10-10-10-K-K.
FLUSH	Any five cards of any value, all in the same suit, but not as a straight or royal flush, e.g., 6-2-K-7-Q all in hearts, diamonds, clubs, or spades.
STRAIGHT	Any five consecutive value cards which are not in the same suit—e.g., 3-4-5-6-7, all off-suit.
THREE OF A KIND	Any three same value cards—e.g., Q-Q-Q.
TWO PAIR	Any two same value cards with any other two same value card—e.g., J-J with 10-10; suits don't matter and the fifth card doesn't matter.
PAIR OF JACKS OR BETTER	Any two jacks, queens, kings, or aces; suits don't matter, and any of the other three cards dealt also don't matter. If they did, you would have a better hand, like some of the hands listed above.

The object of a game of Video Poker, therefore, is to make one of these winning hands. Of course, the royal flush is the biggest prize, but also the hardest to get. The higher the listing, the harder the hands are to make. These payoff schedules appear listed on the front of the machine, usually on a brightly lit glass facade above the actual video screen. The payoffs are listed in five columns, each column corresponding to the number of coins you can play on this particular machine.

Most regular Video Poker machines now available are what we call 9/6 (nine/six) machines. What this means and how this applies to your choices I will explain later. On such a machine the payoffs for a *one-coin* bet will be as follows:

ROYAL FLUSH	250
STRAIGHT FLUSH	50
FOUR OF A KIND	25
FULL HOUSE	9
FLUSH	6
STRAIGHT	4
THREE OF A KIND	3
TWO PAIR	2
PAIR OF JACKS OR BETTER	1

If you hit a winning hand, as listed here, you will be paid that winning amount for a one-coin bet. These payoff amounts are multiplied by each additional coin bet. For example, if you bet three coins and hit a flush, your winnings will be 18 coins. The one exception to this rule comes when you bet five coins and hit the royal flush. If you bet five coins, all winning schedules are multiplied by a factor of 5, but not the royal flush. Instead of just 1,250 coins, the royal flush pays 4,000 coins.

The reason is very simple: this is a bonus amount, designed as an incentive for players to play five coins. Of course, you don't have to play the five coins, but the smart player will always do so, especially on 25-cent video poker machines. The difference between winning $62.50 for a one-coin bet and winning $1,000 is profound, and worth the additional four-coin wager.

The Video Poker phenomenon has become so popular that every manufacturer has tried to improve on the idea. This has given birth to a wide variety of Video Poker machines that are now commonplace in Nevada casinos, as well as in other gaming centers nationwide.

◆| **PROGRESSIVE POKER** |◆

Progressive Video Poker is regular Video Poker with a different payoff schedule and a jackpot shared among several machines. Any one of these machines can hit the top jackpot if that player, betting the five-coin bet, receives the royal flush.

There are two main differences from regular Video Poker: first, the jackpot is not a fixed amount but is a progressive amount, as shown on the "progressive meter." This meter indicates the value of the top jackpot as it rises incrementally—usually by one cent for each dollar that is put through the machines linked to that progressive jackpot. This doesn't sound like much, but the progressive jackpots usually start at $1,000 for the 25-cent machines, and $4,000 for the $1 machines, and—since there are normally about twelve machines per carousel all linked together to one jackpot—very quickly escalate in value.

This jackpot continues to grow play after play after play until a royal flush is hit. But you have to play the maximum coins in order to win the top jackpot, which is the amount the progressive pay meter shows at the moment the royal flush is hit.

The second main difference between progressive and regular Video Poker machines is the slightly lower payoff on some winning hands other than the top jackpot. These progressive Video Poker machines typically are what we call 8/5, rather than the 9/6 norm for nonprogressive machines. The way to tell them apart from regular poker machines is to look at the one-coin payoffs for a full house and flush.

On most regular Video Poker machines the payoff for a full house on a one-coin bet is nine, and the flush six. This is the 9/6 machine. Progressive Video Poker machines are normally 8/5, and therefore the full house pays eight coins for a one-coin bet, and the flush five coins. On a five-coin bet the difference translates to a full house payoff of forty coins, and a flush payoff of twenty-five coins, as opposed to forty-five coins and thirty coins on the regular 9/6 Video Poker machines. Your chances of hitting the royal flush on these 8/5 machines is somewhat diminished, both because they happen slightly less often than with the more liberal 9/6 machines, but also because the smaller, and less frequent, payoffs eat up your bankroll faster than on the 9/6 machines.

These lesser payoffs mean you have fewer credits to play with, therefore fewer chances for winning hands. You'll require a larger bankroll to sustain the same number of hands and playing time that you could otherwise expect from the 9/6 machines. This difference constitutes the House edge, which is built into these machines as a means of paying for the extra money that can be won when the top jackpot is hit. Basically, the odds of winning are slightly lower on these machines than on the regular 9/6 Video Poker machines, but the difference is not great, and will, of course, be more than offset if you are lucky enough to hit the progressive jackpot.

• | OLD-STYLE REGULAR VIDEO POKER | •

When Video Poker machines first came out, their payoffs were set at 6/5. This means thirty coins for a full house with a five-coin bet, and twenty-five coins for the flush. These are the worst odds on any Video Poker machine, so much so that players soon got wise and simply refused to play them. That is why almost all the casinos in Nevada now offer only the 9/6 and the 8/5 versions.

Regular Video Poker 6/5 machines are extremely rare in major Nevada casinos today. Those that remain are mostly the nickel machines, primarily because casinos

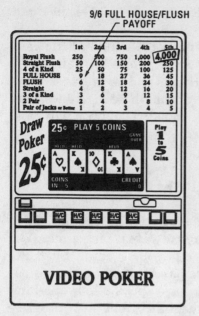

9/6 FULL HOUSE/FLUSH PAYOFF

8/5 FULL HOUSE/FLUSH PAYOFF

6/5 FULL HOUSE/FLUSH PAYOFF

A 9/6 machine, an 8/5 machine, and a 6/5 machine. Note the different payoffs these offer for the same full house and flush hands.

make most of their money in slots from the nickel and quarter players.

Most of these 6/5 dinosaurs can be found in little casinos, bars, restaurants, and supermarkets. A few can also be found in Atlantic City, on riverboats and on Indian gaming reservations. If you ever come across these machines, stay away from them. They will eat you alive and you will most likely regret ever having seen one.

•| BONUS POKER |•

Bonus Poker is another derivative of the regular Video Poker machine. These are almost always 8/5 machines. The major difference in them is the payoff schedule. Such Bonus Poker machines offer extra payoffs if certain combinations are hit, usually a bonus for a specific four-of-a-kind hit. On regular Video Poker machines, and most progressives, a four-of-a-kind (four jacks, four kings, etc.) pays 125 coins for a 5-coin bet. On a Bonus Poker machine the payoffs are divided as follows:

Four 2's, 3's and 4's pay 200 coins for a 5-coin bet.

Four aces pay 400 coins for a 5-coin bet.

Four 5's, 6's, 7's, 8's, 9's, 10's, jacks, queens, and kings pay the regular 125 coins for a 5-coin bet.

The advantage for the player here is that if you hit the Bonus hand, you get paid substantially more than on a regular Poker machine. These machines are quite good to play, and the 8/5 odds are not that bad as Video Poker machines go.

As with the progressives, the slightly worse odds of 8/5 provide for the House edge and allow for the extra payoffs on the bonus hands. The top jackpot on these machines is also the royal flush, which pays 4,000 coins for a 5-coin bet, same as on regular Video Poker. The player's advantage therefore lies in hitting the smaller payoffs and getting paid more for them.

◆| GIMMICK MACHINES |◆

In addition to regular Video Poker, progressive Video Poker, and Bonus Video Poker, several casinos have other versions of this game, usually as a custom exclusive made specifically for one particular casino. There are many casinos who use a variety of these machines. Among the more common are:

Fantastic Fives:

This is an 8/5 machine that pays a bonus if you hit four fives in combination with a jack, queen, king, or ace as the fifth card. The payoff for a 5-coin bet is 4,000 coins for four fives with an ace, just like the royal flush; less for four fives with a king; less with a queen; less with a jack; and the regular 125 coins for anything else.

Straight Flush Rush:

This is the same kind of machine as the Fantastic Fives, but this time the bonus payoff is on specific straight flush hands. Spade straight flush pays a bonus, as do hearts, diamonds, and clubs, in much the same hierarchy as the Fantastic Fives.

Bonus Sevens:

Again the same principle, but you get paid 250 coins if you hit four sevens, regardless of what you have with them as the fifth card. Another variation is Bonus Nines. Still others employ a bonus on specific flush hands, like "diamonds."

Jumping Jacks:

These are the same as the Bonus Sevens, except you get 600 coins if you hit four jacks.

I call all these machines gimmick machines because that's exactly what they are. Mostly they are designed to eat your money. Stay away from them, and play the Bonus Poker, progressives, or regular Video Poker. You'll typically score more winning hands, allowing you more playing time—time and play to possibly hit "the big one."

Reversible Royals:

These can be found in various versions in most casinos. Their distinction is that if, on a five-coin bet, you hit a royal flush in sequence, that is: A-K-Q-J-10, or 10-J-Q-K-A, you win the bonus—$12,500 for a 25-cent machine, $50,000 for a $1 machine and, on some, $250,000 for a $5 machine.

But don't hold your breath. It's hard enough to hit the royal flush, much less to get it in sequence. It does happen, but the incredibly high payoffs should indicate to you just how tough it is to get this hand. And some casinos only pay this version one way, say 10 through ace, and not the other way around, further compounding the difficulty of winning it.

One of these monster Royals did hit for $250,000 at the Palace Station Hotel/Casino in Las Vegas, and it was quite a publicity coup for the resort. For several weeks the marquee outside the hotel proclaimed congratulations to the winner. I share the sentiment, but unless you are *extremely* wealthy I will never recommend that you try to play these machines just to hit this kind of a super jackpot. The chances of winning it are incredibly small.

These Video Poker machines are usually 8/5 machines, and some are even Bonus Poker machines. They are not that bad to play, but if you are going to play them, remember *not* to play *just to hit the reversible royal flush,* or you'll go broke very quickly. Play them as you normally would for all the payoffs available; and, if you're really lucky, you might be dealt the reversible royal. If you are, thank your lucky stars, pat yourself on the back for making the right choice, and pocket your bonus winnings.

Deuces Wild

Probably the most popular variation on Video Poker yet invented, Deuces Wild is a game that employs the 2-value card (called deuce) as a "wild" card. Being wild means that the deuce can play as any other card, depending on what best improves your hand. For instance, one king and one deuce becomes a pair of kings, one deuce and three aces will make four aces, and so on. The deuce therefore can be used to make any kind of Poker hand: straight, flush, full house, four-of-a-kind, five-of-a-kind, etc.—even the royal flush. When playing Deuces Wild machines it is important to remember that these machines begin to pay off only on three-of-a-kind or better, and *not* pair of jacks or better. This is because the wild deuces make more winning combinations more often.

A regular deck of fifty-two cards will have four of each value card, including four deuces. On a Deuces Wild Video Poker game, these deuces will not only allow you to make many more paying hands much more frequently, but can also win you the second-highest jackpot. As is the case with all Video Poker machines, the royal flush is the highest jackpot. But on a Deuces Wild machine, the four deuces also offer a nice jackpot.

On regular Video Poker machines a four-of-a-kind will pay 125 coins for a 5-coin bet; but four deuces on a Deuces Wild machine will pay 1,000 coins for a 5-coin bet. This, of course, is in addition to all the other hands you can make by using the wild deuces as help. The catch is that, outside the jackpots, the overall payoffs, with or without the deuces, are much smaller than on either regular Video Poker machines or bonus machines. For instance: a full house will pay 45 coins for a 5-coin bet on a regular 9/6 machine, 40 coins for a 5-coin bet on the 8/5 machines, but only 15 coins on the Deuces Wild machine.

There are two main reasons for this. One is that the four wild deuces in the deck allow the player to make many more winning hands than would be possible on regular Video Poker, which uses no wild cards. The other is the House edge, that extra few coins the House withholds from the payoff schedule in order to make up for the extra money paid out when you hit the four deuces. It is also important to remember that if you hit a royal flush and you used one or more wild deuces to make that winning hand, you will *not* get the top jackpot. The top jackpot *is* the royal flush, which pays 4,000 coins for a 5-coin bet, but *only* if you get it *without* using any deuce to help. A lot of people get very excited when hitting a so-called "Wild Royal," only to be disappointed when they realize it does not win them the top jackpot but only 125 coins for a 5-coin bet.

Deuces Wild machines are fun to play . . . but be careful. There are quite a few different versions of Deuces Wild available, and not all pay the same. Look for a machine that pays 25 coins for a four-of-a-kind with a 5-coin bet, with or without the deuces. These are the best odds now available on Deuces Wild machines, and they are typically 9/5. You may also refer to the Wild Royal payoff schedule on the machine's payoff display to see if it pays 125 coins for a 5-coin bet. This is also one of the better machines. The best machines overall are those that have both of these payoffs listed.

Some casinos employ a gimmick variation on Deuces Wild called Triple Pay Deuces Wild. These machines will pay $750 (3,000 coins) on a 25-cent machine for the four deuces, as opposed to the $250 (1,000 coins) normally found on 25-cent Deuces Wild machine. These gimmick machines pay only 100 coins for a Wild Royal on a 5-coin bet, 20 coins for a four of a kind and only 50 coins (instead of the normal 75 coins) for a five of a kind. The principle is the same, but the four deuces on these triple-pay machines are much harder to hit because of the terrible odds offered—generally 8/4—and you do not get many smaller payoffs to keep you playing. I certainly do not recommend playing this kind of machine.

Jokers Wild

Similar to Deuces Wild, Jokers Wild machines are usually 7/5 machines that use a standard 52-card deck, plus one joker. This joker works the same as the deuces, but there is only one in the deck. The top jackpot is, again, the royal flush without the joker, then the five-of-a-kind, the joker royal, and the four-of-a-kind.

Based on a 5-coin bet, five-of-a-kind pays 1,000 coins, and to get it you must get four of a kind *and* the joker all together on the screen at the same time. Royal flush with joker will pay 500 coins, and the royal flush without joker 4,000 coins.

These machines are popular and fun to play, but they can get expensive. The 7/5 odds are not that good, and the schedule of payoffs is also quite poor. But it is possible to win more often on Jokers Wild than on the gimmick machines. Some Jokers Wild machines will offer a top jackpot of 4,700 coins for the royal flush without joker, and these are the machines you should look for. However, I would not recommend playing them too often. They can eat up the change and some players have dubbed them the "Hoover machines," meaning they are the vacuum cleaners of video poker and will suck up your bankroll.

◆| VIDEO POKER ODDS AND PERCENTAGES |◆

Video Poker machines are based on a computer. The game they play is a software program, written to specific rules and designed to pay out winning hands every certain number of hands played. The payoff schedule is based on an annual average of constant play, a computer-simulation test-case average over 1 million hands.

As a rule of thumb, a 9/6 machine will pay out 96 percent of all the money put through the machine over a period of one year, based on constant play with maximum coins bet each time. The same principle holds for the rest of the machines: 8/5 pays out 85 percent, 7/5 pays out 75 percent and 6/5 pays out 65 percent. These loose percentages more or less reflect payoffs in the real world, where mistake-ridden play by most players drastically reduces the true payoffs that can theoretically be achieved. In theory, and with perfect play, the true payoffs are closer to 99 percent for a 9/6 machine, 95 percent to 97 percent for 8/5 and 7/5 machines, and 92 percent for the 6/5 machines, especially the very old ones.

An extremely important point to remember is that these payoff percentages do *not* mean that for every $1 you put in on a 9/6 machine you will get back ninety-nine cents, or even ninety-six cents. This is a common misconception among casual players.

Some Video Poker machines can, in fact, be played to a 101 percent payback, but this means absolutely perfect play on each and every hand over the life of the payoff cycle. Perfect play means holding and drawing cards for the *most likely payout* on each hand and not taking any long shots for bigger payoffs. For instance, most players would throw away one pair of kings to go for a royal flush when four-to-the-royal—four of the necessary five cards that make up a royal flush—are dealt on the screen, with the odd card being the extra king. However, perfect play would dictate that you keep the two kings and draw for the three or four kings, or for the two pair and full house options, always mindful of the fact you already have a paying hand. Playing the machines this way with consistent five-coin play will, over the life of the payoff cycle, offer the player a 1 percent edge over the house.

So if you play a quarter machine an average of four hands per minute (easily done on Video Poker machines), it gives you an expense of $5.00 per minute (five coins per bet with quarters), which equals 240 hands per hour, adding up to $300 per hour, $7,200 per 24-hour day, and $2,628,000 per 365-day year. You can expect to make $26,280 per year as your 1 percent edge, playing a 25-cent 9/6 machine, five coins per bet, with perfect play.

Don't rush out and start thinking you can make a living at it. Even Superman sleeps and eats sometimes, and if you averaged twelve hours per day of perfect play, you would still make only half that total money. And what if you made a mistake? Just one mistake is all it would take to ruin this entire perfect play principle and you would have to start that cycle all over again.

When I speak of a payoff cycle, I am referring to the frequency with which the machines will hit the various pays, including the jackpot pays. For instance, on the average, a 9/6 regular Video Poker machine with no wild cards will hit the royal flush once each 40,000 hands played. But this does not mean that each machine will pay the jackpot royal flush each 40,000 hands like clockwork. Remember, the machines are set, by law, to select winning combinations at *random*.

How can a machine that selects winning combinations at random still pay the jackpot each 40,000 hands played? Very simply, the computer program has a master control chip which, in layman's terms, has two main divisions. One selects the cards that will be dealt at random, and the second acts as master control, making sure that winning hands conform to the overall program schedule of payoff frequency. In effect, the master control rides shotgun over the random selections.

This is at best a metaphorical explanation, but it is basically accurate for the purpose of illustration. The master control does not function in specific sequences. Yes, it does carry in its program a schedule that says, "Pay royal flush each 40,000 hands," but it is averaged over the annual life of the machine's cycle. In reality, any given machine can hit royal flushes back to back, or even several times in one day. But then it will not hit the royal flush again until enough hands are played to bring the cycle back into line. So, whatever happens, in the end the *average* will be one royal flush each 40,000 hands. And the same applies proportionately to all the other pays on the payoff schedule.

This principle applies to all slot machines, whether computerized or not. But since most machines these days are computerized, it is even more important to know, and remember, what payoffs and payoff percentages really mean and how they apply to your chances of winning.

• | SIMPLE STRATEGY FOR VIDEO POKER | •

Video Poker machines use a standard 52-card deck, shuffled electronically after each hand is played. The machines are set, by law, to randomly select the first five cards dealt to the player at the beginning of each hand, followed by a second set of five cards that the machine keeps in check, unseen by the player, until the player makes a selection of which of the first five cards he will hold and which he will throw away. It makes absolutely no difference which cards the player holds and which he throws away. The second set of five cards is predetermined, and the machine will deal these cards, and only these cards, for the duration of the current game.

If, for instance, you chose to keep two of the five cards you were dealt initially, the machine will then deal you the first three of the other five cards it picked, in that order.

Example: You are dealt: A-K-K-10-8 (forget the suits for now)

This means you already have a winner. The pair of kings will automatically pay you even money. But the object is to improve the hand and win more, right?

So you press the hold button under each of the kings to hold those cards on the screen, and after you hit the deal button the machine will throw away the other three cards and deal you three new cards.

Example: 7-K-6

Now the hand is finished, and you have improved your hand from a mere even-money pair to a three of a kind: the three kings. This will then pay you fifteen coins for a five-coin bet, as opposed to the five coins you would have won if you had kept all the five cards originally dealt to you. That is the advantage of Video Poker; it offers you a choice in what you do and how you do it.

Of course, if no other king appears and no other pair, or no other winning combination, you are still left with that pair of kings and still get your 5 coins back.

For any novice player, the simplest advice that I can offer is: *Never throw away a winning hand.* If the machine deals you a winner on the first five cards dealt, don't throw it away hoping to catch a better winner. Keep it, throw away the rest of the cards and try to improve the hand you have been dealt. You'll get the idea after you have played a few hands.

The *only* exception is if you have been dealt four cards to the royal flush, or an open-end straight flush. A draw to an open-end straight flush means a set of four cards of the same suit that can be made into a straight flush by drawing one card either as the high card or as the low card. For example: 6-7-8-9 all in hearts is an open-end straight flush draw, because it allows you to make the straight flush either by drawing the ten of hearts as the high card, or by drawing the five of hearts as the low card. Payoffs for the straight flush and the royal flush are so much bigger than anything else that it is worth the risk of throwing away the one odd card in hopes of being dealt the one card you still need to make this big winner.

Choice comes into play again when selecting which Video Poker machine you will play. By now you should have a fairly good idea of which types of machines are better than others. But there are some other considerations you should keep in mind.

Remember the payoff percentage in making your selection. Never forget this, and never forget to look at the payoff display before you sit down to play. It bears repeating, because it is very important. Should you sit down at a regular Video Poker machine whose payoff schedule is 8/5 and it offers no bonus pays and it is not a progressive, you *must* be aware of what you're getting and what you're giving up in playing it.

In simplest terms, playing such a non-bonus non-progressive machine means you give up five coins for each full house and five coins for each flush. Over your playing session this will amount to a sizable loss. Of course, if this machine *is* either a bonus pay machine or a progressive, the loss will be offset if you hit the top jackpot royal flush or any extra bonus pays on a bonus pay machine.

Never throw away a winner if it is dealt to you, unless you have a one-card draw to the top jackpot. Even then think twice about it.

As you are playing your machine, see how it is playing. If it is dealing you lots of pairs, chances are you will improve a pair. If it has not dealt you a flush for some time, chances are the cycle is about to determine a flush hand, so go for it. But many machines will tease you with several four-to-the-royal hands and, when you go for this jackpot, will not give it to you.

Therefore, if you constantly throw away winning pairs to draw to the royal, chances are you will go broke very quickly. That is why your judgment in playing Video Poker is important, as are your powers of observation. If your machine is teasing you like this, it will almost never hit the jackpot.

From direct personal experience, and from that of many players I know, I can absolutely vouch that in the real world of casino Video Poker, royal flush jackpots almost always hit unexpectedly. Virtually all such jackpots have hit for me and for the players I know specifically when the machine *did not* show such royal flush draws. In fact, most of the time, royal flush jackpots hit when the machine suddenly appears to be playing poorly, and seems to start taking money from you and not hit any payoffs at all.

Some die-hard Video Poker players will tell you that it is best to play machines at the end of the rows nearest the aisle where there's a lot of foot traffic. As far as superstitions go, this one is as good as another. But an argument can be made for its validity. If the casinos wanted to, and could, alter the payoff percentage and cycle on Video Poker machines, it would serve them well to make the end-of-the-row machines pay out more often. The logic behind this is simple. If such a machine did pay off more, more people would be seeing the winners because of the machine's high-visibility location. Seeing people winning on this machine would entice others to sit at available machines and play them. And the more people that play, the more money the casino makes.

This is a reasonable superstition, but a superstition nonetheless. Nevada casinos cannot change odds and payoff percentages on their machines without the approval of the Gaming Control Board, and, in any case, the casino would only be allowed to change the kind of machine they provide and not the programming chip inside. For instance, if the casino wished to offer Video Poker machines with a higher House withholding percentage, they would have to do so by changing them from, say, 9/6 machines to 8/5.

However, many players still swear that these end-of-the-row machines pay out more and do so more often. And on some, it is in fact true—but not because they are set to pay more. The simple explanation is that they pay out more because they are played more. Because they are next to high-traffic thoroughfares, they are selected more often by passing players. Consequently, since all machines pay off on prespecified cycles based on the number of hands played, the more hands that are played on such end-of-the-row machines the more often these machines will pay out. The cycle and percentages remain the same, but the ideal location of such machines means that they usually get more play and therefore *seem* to pay out more money more often.

As a result, one helpful hint I can offer is to look for high-traffic areas where the machines get lots of play. Of course this will not assure you of picking just the right one. Gambling is just that: gambling. This means you take a chance. But you can get lucky and pick a machine that will pay you on the first five coins you put in. I've seen it happen. Then again, you may sit down at a machine that has just paid off and won't pay the top jackpot again for some time. But you can take a calculated chance simply by keeping your eyes open. Such *informed choice* will get you further with your gaming dollars.

One way to help yourself is to ask. Every casino has many change people around. These employees walk around the casino, usually in bright, easy-to-spot uniforms, selling change to players. Assigned to specific areas of the casino, they stand by the very same machines day after day, shift after shift, for an average of eight hours each shift.

They see it all. Ask if they know whether the machine you want to play has hit recently, or if it has had a lot of play. Most of the time these change people will be more than glad to offer their opinions. They are still only opinions, but usually informed ones based on observations made over a long period of time. Some casinos encourage their employees to offer this kind of help and others tolerate it; few actually forbid it. In any case, it is mostly up to the people you ask whether or not they will offer the advice.

If they do, and the advice is good, don't forget to tip them well if you win. Their minimum wage is supplemented by such tips, an incentive for them to be nice to players. Such information is helpful, but in the end the choice becomes yours. Try the recommended machine. If it does well, stay. If not, find a better one to play.

Casinos place Video Poker machines in all different areas around the casino floor. Some machines are straight-up types, where you sit in front of them and look straight ahead into the screen. Others are what is known as "slant tops," where you sit down and look down at the machine whose screen is on a slight angle in front of you. It makes no difference to the performance of the machine. Slant tops are, however, more comfortable to sit at and play.

Another simple bit of advice is always to check carefully the type of Video Poker machine you are about to play. Machines are arranged in groups, called carousels, but all the machines in a carousel do not have to be the same. They may all *look* the same, but beware. Often a carousel of Video Poker machines can have several different types all there together and all looking the same. This is a trap for the unwary. One machine may be a 9/6, while the one immediately next to it can be an 8/5, or even 6/5.

Be a smart player. Look at the payout display, either on the machine itself, or on the video display payoff schedule on the machine's screen. Pay attention to what you see and apply what you have learned. Otherwise you could be unpleasantly surprised when your payoff is less than you expected. As I explained earlier, a good rule of thumb is never to play a 6/5 machine—*never!*

And don't play an 8/5 unless it is either a progressive or a Bonus Poker machine. Don't be fooled by advertising that reads "98% payout" when it appears over a carousel of Video Poker machines if these machines are 6/5 or nonprogressive or nonbonus 8/5 machines. It doesn't matter what the advertising says—if it's a 6/5 machine it will eat you up! If it's an 8/5 machine that is neither linked to a progressive meter for the top jackpot nor offering Bonus Poker, playing it will always cost you more money than you can reasonably expect to recover from well-paying hands. There are virtually no rules for in-casino advertising. Do you believe everything you see advertised on TV? Of course not, and neither should you believe advertising you see for gambling payoffs, whether in print or on the casino floor. Indeed, in order to comply with fair advertising practices and prevent any form of false advertising law suits, all any advertiser has to do, casinos included, is offer one—just one—product that fully complies with advertised claims.

Applied to casinos, this simply means that if the casino advertises a 98 percent payout over any given carousel of machines, it really needs to have only one machine in the entire carousel which pays off at that rate. *Every* casino in Las Vegas, Atlantic City, Reno, or any major gaming center, offers Video Poker machines. However not all casinos will offer the same type of machines, or offer the better-odds 9/6 machines. And some casinos offer better progressives than others. In general, if you decide to play regular Video Poker, go to a casino that offers the 9/6 machines, and look for one that has been played a lot and has not hit a royal flush recently. As a general rule, this will improve your chances of winning.

There is also a huge difference between the kind of Video Poker machines you will find in casinos outside Nevada. Nevada has been the pace-setter in legalized gambling for many decades, and perhaps for that reason the newest and most liberal games are found there. For instance, Atlantic City casinos used to offer only 6/5 and 7/5 Video Poker machines. Only recently did they upgrade their machines to the more liberal 8/5, but that is still far behind Nevada. And the 8/5 machines in Atlantic City are mostly half-dollar and dollar machines, although quarter machines are now also being made available to East Coast gamblers. These are slim pickings for Video Poker players.

In defense of Atlantic City, this situation is largely the result of the extremely strict gaming regulations imposed by the New Jersey Gaming Commission, regulations that allowed little room for gaming innovation. Fortunately this is changing rapidly. As gaming finds more and more acceptance among the voters and the general public, elected officials are beginning to respond. For many years gaming agencies, such as the Nevada and New Jersey Gaming commissions, have been the appointed watchdogs, making sure that organized crime did not infiltrate legalized gaming or dominate it as it had from the 1940s to the 1970s. With the fear of Mob control finally laid to rest, appointed regulatory agencies are allowing Atlantic City casino operators more room for innovation. The direct result has been a greater variety of games for the players, and games offering better payoffs, such as 9/6 Video Poker.

By far the worst payoffs for Video Poker play are to be found in the new casinos now sprouting in the Midwest, on Indian reservations, riverboats, and the old gold-mining ghost towns currently being converted to gaming resorts. These gambling centers offer 6/5 machines almost exclusively, with very few offering 7/5 and 8/5 machines. If you go to play at these destinations, be aware of what you're getting. Then you can play accordingly.

But this situation is also changing, and soon most of these new gaming resorts will also offer the better variety of Video Poker machines for their customers.

My final piece of advice for Video Poker is: *if* you play at all, then *play to win!* And this means that you should always play the maximum coin bet. You must remember that if you do not play the maximum coin bet, you will *never* win the top jackpot. By playing maximum coins you reduce the House edge because you are in the running to win the 4,000 coin royal flush jackpot. This payoff is considerably higher than all the other little payoffs combined.

Don't shortchange yourself. Betting only one or two coins at a time rather than maximum coins is a prescription for disaster. Many people do it constantly, and they are simply throwing their money away and enriching the casino owner. Playing this way you will *never* win the top-paying jackpot, and whatever little pays you get along the way will almost never pay for the money you spent playing. I'm very serious about this. If all you intend to do is play one, two, three or four coins at a time, stay home, go to a movie or go bowling. Playing this way will make your gambling vacation an exercise in frustration.

Before you go to gamble, always determine how much money you are willing to spend. No, this is not admitting that you are going out to lose. It is simply budgeting what you decide your entertainment will cost you. Your bankroll is the gauge by which you should determine which machines you will play and how long you will play them. On the average, $200 is a good bankroll for some serious play on quarter Video Poker machines: 9/6 regular, 8/5 progressive or 8/5 Bonus Poker. Twice that, or $400, is recommended if you plan to play $1 machines; $1,500 to $3,000 for $5 machines—for those that take five coins per pull—less for those taking only three coins per pull; and a whole lot more if you plan to spend several hours at a $25 or $100 Video Poker machine.

Another important factor that applies to all gambling is: How much is enough? This is largely determined by what the value of your money is to you at that given time. If you don't care about spending what you brought and what you won, to hell with it. Go for broke. However, if you want to take some of your money home with you, then set a limit. What if you *do* hit the top jackpot on your Video Poker machine? Is that enough? It should be. Put it away and play another day. And what if you don't hit the top jackpot, but are winning a lot of smaller pays? A good rule to follow is: If you have doubled your money, it's enough. Take it and go. Perhaps play another machine, but don't get hooked.

Many machines are teasers. They will *almost* give you the big jackpot. In the process they may even pay out quite a few smaller jackpots. Apply the "double my money" principle. If you've done it, take it, go home, or at least go play another machine and begin a new session.

2
SLOT MACHINES

Games of chance are as old as history itself. It can be argued that gambling is the world's oldest profession (beating out that obvious one). Even Adam gambled when he bit into the apple offered by Eve because he wanted to find out what he'd get if he did it. Of course we all know how that turned out. . . .

Gambling machines, however, are a more contemporary invention. During the industrial revolution of the nineteenth century, machines were invented to do a variety of tasks previously done by manpower, or work previously impossible. Cunning minds soon began to find ways they could apply this new mechanical technology to games. Roulette and the big wheel are perhaps the oldest applications of machines to gambling. But in all honesty these games are not quite the kind of gambling machines we now know as slot machines.

One of the oldest slot machines was one made around 1906, and was a variation on the big wheel. The big wheel, which can be found in almost all modern casinos, is a large wheel mounted vertically, like a wagon wheel, with spikes protruding from one face arranged along the edge, and with numbers marked on the wheel between the spikes.

The game is played by spinning the wheel, and the players bet on which number a "rabbit's foot"—firmly mounted just above the wheel—will end up over once the wheel stops. Most people have probably seen one. It looks something like a Ferris wheel. It is similar to the wheel used in the TV game show "Wheel of Fortune," except that the one on the game show is horizontal.

This same principle was applied at the turn of the century in a primitive machine that used three large wheels mounted side by side with coin slots for the bets and a handle to pull to start the wheels spinning. In effect, this was the granddaddy of the slot machine. It is a very interesting contraption, and one is on display at the Rio Hotel and Casino in Las Vegas.

Like all mechanical gadgets, the slot machine evolved over the years. It probably gained its notoriety as "the one-armed bandit" during the Prohibition era of the 1920s and 1930s, when the Chicago gangs (and gangs all over the country) used them as part of their illicit operations. Indeed, in the old TV series "The Untouchables," there are a few episodes where you see Eliot Ness and his men bust up these old slots.

The first legitimate use of slot machines in America appeared when Las Vegas was born as the gambling capital of the world, after Bugsy Siegel built the old Flamingo and installed slot machines among the games offered in his casino. Other hotels followed, and as Las Vegas gained popularity, more slots were added as a pastime for the gamblers. These old slots were mechanical monsters, mostly with three and four reels, and their principle was based on weighted reels that were supposed to come up with random combinations of symbols. As is the case with slot machines today, the object was to line up three or more matching symbols on the pay line in order to get a winner.

Of course these old slots were easily tampered with and subject to play with "slugs" (phoney money tokens); they were also poor payers, and were for the most part dismissed with disdain by gamblers as silly diversions.

Times change. As with Video Poker, the invention of computer technology, computer chips, and ever more sophisticated software programs, coupled with the increased awareness by casino owners of the tremendous profit potential of slot machines, eventually led to the emergence of the slot machine as the prime gambling attraction of the latter half of the twentieth century.

Today the slot machine boasts more varieties than ice cream. Increasingly sophisticated computer programs, graphics, and sound effects have made the slot machine the up-to-date friend of the modern gambler. No longer reliant on clumsy, clanging mechanical reels, slot machines today are smooth devices, and some are merely computer displays on a video screen. They are brightly painted and have catchy names like: Red, White, and Blue; Slam Dunk; Home Run; Wild Cherries; Bonus Sevens; and so on.

Although there are almost more varieties of reel slots than you can imagine, all still work on the same principle as the old slots. You put a coin, or two or three or four or five (or sometimes even more) in the slot and pull the handle (or push the button, on these modern contraptions), the reels spin, and if the "pay" symbols are lined up on the machine's display payline, you win. If not, you lose. Payoffs are determined by the hierarchical scale clearly charted on the machine's display.

Slots are the simplest game to play, although some of the more ambitious slots can seem a trifle complicated. But don't be overwhelmed by the graphics, displays, or the apparent complexity of a modern slot machine. No matter how complicated it looks, it still works the same as every other slot machine. Line up the paying combinations on the win line and you win.

Modern slot machines work on a computer program similar to that in a Video Poker machine: random selection of winning combinations, based on a program command that determines the overall payout and take of such a machine over a period of one year. Winning percentages and odds are set by the manufacturer as part of the software program of the slot machine, and are calculated by millions of spins made with computer simulations. As with Video Poker, a modern slot machine will pay off the top jackpot each certain number of spins. The number and frequency of such wins is determined by the payout percentage built into the program of that particular machine.

Unlike in Video Poker, however, the player has no choice in the matter and cannot affect the winning combinations. The slot machine is, therefore, a passive game, and not an interactive one. Although quite rare, there are some "second chance" reel slots; however, even these are not truly interactive in the same sense as Video Poker.

The popularity of slot machines has increased steadily over the past two decades, largely as a result of increasing computer sophistication, but also because computers, computer games, video arcade games, and other electronically generated and interactive games have become part of the American lifestyle.

◆ HOW, WHAT, AND WHY OF SLOT MACHINES ◆

On one of my frequent visits to the Stardust Hotel/Casino on the Las Vegas Strip I was attracted to a specific carousel of slot machines. These 25-cent slots offer a brand-new luxury car as the top prize. The cars are always in the $40,000-plus range—Mercedes, Jaguars, top-line Cadillacs, and so on. This night a beautiful Mercedes, worth some $50,000, was the prize. Since I needed a new car, I thought, "Why go buy one? Let's win one!" So I sat down with my bucket of quarters and merrily began a six-hour odyssey. I won just about everything on the board *except* the top prize. By then I was tired and thought I'd go and take a shower before returning.

About half an hour later I went back to the casino to continue and ran into Frank Regich, my friend and casino host. Frank was all excited. I asked why, but I didn't have to. As soon as I saw the crowd around *my machine*, I knew it! Yes, it had hit the big one.

It seems the lady who won the prize had just come out of Tony Roma's restaurant, and her husband had three quarters in his pocket, so he gave them to her to play in a machine as they passed by. Well, what do you know! It was *my* machine, *one pull* after I left it, and the happy couple drove home to Illinois in style.

Yes, this lucky player was *very* lucky. But a smart slot player could have made the same choice. I had played that slot machine for a long time, thousands of spins, and I was getting good pays. It was weariness that contributed to my loss of the top jackpot. I won money overall but did not win the big jackpot. As a smart player, when I was beginning to get tired I took the money I had won and went for some rest. Another smart player, observing my play, could have stepped up to that same machine and hit the jackpot.

All it takes is the knowledge to make smart and well-informed choices—choices designed to help your luck along. In any gambling game, particularly in slots, luck is an important element. But if you know something about slot machines, how they are set and why they play and pay the way they do, it will help you choose what to play. And you will know *why* you chose to play that particular machine and suddenly seem to be one of the lucky players. As with the man at the Mirage who turned a few dollars into $5.6 million, it can happen to you.

In this chapter, "how" will show you how to play, how much to bet, and some simple strategy. "What" refers to what machines to play, what kind of machines there are, and which are better than others. "Why" explains why some machines pay more, why it is better to play certain kinds of machines, and why you should bet a specific amount of money.

◆| HOW |◆

In case you have never played a slot machine or have not played some of the newer slot machines lately, I shall begin by describing how you start.

Players begin play by inserting a specified number of coins, or gaming tokens, into a coin-receptacle slot provided on the front of the machine, and then pulling the handle affixed to the right side of the machine, which sets the reels spinning. The reels come to a stop in order left to right on the display screen. The object is to line up matching symbols (matching winning combinations) on the payline, usually a center stripe painted across the viewing screen. The schedule of winning combinations is usually displayed on the front or just above the machine, indicating the hierarchy of winning combinations and the amounts that each one pays whenever it appears on the active payline.

Instead of a handle, some modern machines employ a button marked "spin," which you press to start the reels turning after the coin, or coins, are inserted. Most modern slot machines, like the Video Poker machines, also have a button marked "credit."

If the player presses this button prior to inserting coins, instead of paying winners off in coins, the machine will automatically credit any winnings to a credit meter. The credited winnings appear numerically on the machine's credit meter display, and, as an option, the player then has a choice of playing these credits or cashing them out. To play the credits, the player can press a button marked "play one credit," and for each time this button is pressed the machine will deduct one credit from the credit meter and register one corresponding coin as "coin in." The player may press the "play one credit" button up to the machine's maximum-coin limit. If, for instance, the machine you are playing takes three coins as maximum, you can press the "play one coin" button three times. These coins are then deducted from the player's credit meter, and credited to the player's next pull. When this is done, the machine will usually say "coin accepted" on the display, or, in some cases, the paylines on the machine's display will light up. The effect is the same as if you had put three coins in the slot instead of using the credits you had accumulated. Most of the modern machines also have another button called "play maximum coins," sometimes also identified as "play 3 coins" if that machine's maximum is three coins, or "play 5 coins" if that machine's maximum is five, and so on. By pressing this button, the player will automatically play the maximum coins that that machine takes.

The player may also cash out these credits by pressing a button marked "collect." When a player presses this button, the machine will pay out in coins, or gaming tokens, all the credits indicated on the credit meter. The coins then drop to the tray mounted at the bottom of the machine.

♦| WHAT AND WHY |♦

What is a slot machine?

A slot machine is a mechanical device employing three, four, five, or more circular reels of varying dimensions. Each of these reels has several symbols either painted on or attached to it. The symbols can be anything at all, although the most common designs are cherries, bars, and—

the jackpot symbol—the number 7. Whatever the symbol on the machine, it makes absolutely no difference in how the machine plays or what and how much it will pay out. All these details are determined by the computer program carried by a tiny chip inside the machine's electronic brain. You could put pictures of your kids, rocks, spaghetti, cheese, or anything there, and, if they lined up on the payline, you'd win the top jackpot.

My examples may appear silly, but the point is important. Many people think that machines with certain symbols will pay better, and casino owners capitalize on this by creating "theme machines." Theme machines are machines with specific gimmicks. For example, some machines have as their displays the various signs of the Zodiac, and the come-on is that a lot of people read horoscopes and so will want to play a machine with their particular symbols, or those of their relatives or friends. It's a popular concept.

Other theme machines are the very popular Red, White, and Blue 7's machines, which trade on American patriotism. Others use football, basketball, baseball, the jungle, fruits, animals, jokers, playing cards, and so on. These themes provide for a variety of looks and lots of bright lights, but, nevertheless, all are *exactly* the same, except for these graphics. You should not play any slot machine just because you like the symbols painted on the reels. There are far smarter ways to make your playing choice.

✦ THREE REELS VERSUS FOUR REELS ✦

Common sense should dictate that it is far easier to line up three matching symbols for a slot machine win than four. To get four of anything is very hard, even on liberal Video Poker.

On a reel slot machine, three 7's can be achieved much more often than four 7's on a four-reel machine. Look for three-reel machines to play.

♦ | **PROGRESSIVE SLOTS** | ♦

Progressive slot machines are usually four-reel machines, although recent trends are toward three-reel machines. As in progressive Video Poker, progressive slot machines offer an open-ended jackpot that increases in value after each pull on every machine within a linked group. The top jackpot can be won *only* if the maximum number of coins is played and all of the winning symbols correctly line up on the pay line. The linked machines are generally grouped together in a carousel, but there are even statewide progressive systems in Nevada that electronically link together machines in different casinos across the state. These jackpots grow fast and are very big when hit. And when the jackpot hits, it may very well not be in the casino in which you are playing, or even in the city in which you are playing. Progressive reel slots are usually dollar machines with a three-coin maximum. Many casinos also offer their own progressives, which can take anything from quarters to $25-dollar tokens, but virtually all take three coins per pull and almost all have four reels. And you *must* play the maximum coins to have a chance at the top jackpot.

You can go through a lot of money playing $3 per pull, especially on these progressives, which do not pay off very often. Even if you do hit some of the smaller pays on the progressives, you still will wind up in the poorhouse if you sit there for any length of time.

My simple advice is, if you want to play a progressive, pick one whose primary and secondary jackpots are at a high level, buy $100 worth of dollar tokens, and play with those. If you lose it, go play the better-odds two-coin three-reel machines. If you win, practice the double-your-money principle. By that I mean, if you have won twice the money you started with and have not hit the top jackpot, take what you won and leave; this is the best way to avoid a long losing streak, and it gives you a greater stake at your next session. And, if you are so very lucky and you do hit the top jackpot, let's hope you have twenty years of life left to collect and the patience to go with it.

Most progressives offer these "primary" and "secondary" jackpots. A primary jackpot is the top prize offered when a player hits the specific combination that will pay the top jackpot. This top jackpot is the one paying the most money, and is usually displayed with the biggest sign and numbers.

A secondary jackpot is a smaller progressive jackpot that pays off when the winning symbols show up together anywhere in the pay window, though not necessarily all lined up on the same pay line. A pay window is the clear see-through glass or plastic area on the front of the machine that allows you to see the spinning reels and the combinations they come up with at the end of each spin. The secondary jackpot payoff is usually displayed on a smaller screen mounted below the big screen for the primary jackpot, and it also increases proportionately to the number of coins played. These jackpots are hit more frequently and therefore do not always have a large sum of money on the progressive meter.

All progressive slots display a progressive meter with digital readout either on the machine itself or over a carousel of such progressive machines. Before playing, check the meter for the primary and secondary jackpots, and compare it against other machines of this type to see how high these jackpots are relative to their starting amounts. Choose those machines that display both primary and secondary jackpots in high amounts. Because the pay meter automatically resets to the base amount once the jackpot is hit, the fact that the jackpots are so high indicates that these machines have had a lot of play without having hit either jackpot.

Therefore, the chances of that jackpot hitting soon are all the greater and your chances of being the lucky player are likewise greater. On the famous Megabucks machines, for example, the primary jackpot begins at $3 million and grows from there; the secondary jackpot starts at $5,000.00. So if you see a Megabucks machine whose primary jackpot is close to $3 million with the secondary jackpot near $5,000, you know they have been hit recently. Save your money and don't play it until the jackpot grows.

The same principle applies to other progressive slots. Some start their primary jackpots at $1,000.00, with a secondary jackpot beginning at $500.00. If you see one of these machines where the primary jackpot is $2,350.00, for example, you know it has not been hit for some time, and this machine therefore becomes a good candidate for your investment. You can, of course, target just one of the jackpots at a time. For example, you may see a progressive machine where the top jackpot has been hit recently, but the secondary jackpot has climbed to near $1,000.00. This machine would still be a good candidate for your money because you know the secondary jackpot has not hit for some time and is likely to do so soon. On the other hand, that same machine may have a secondary jackpot of only $550.00, so you know it has been hit recently; but in this case you should be after the primary jackpot, if it's an attractive one.

If you don't know what the starting value on such machines is, feel free to ask the change person or the floor person, who will be glad to tell you. If that particular machine is near its starting jackpot value, find another like it with a high meter value for the jackpots, or find another progressive. There are so many for you to choose from that you are certain to find one that looks like a winner. But don't start sticking your money in the slots and feeding the meter just because you like the look of the symbols.

♦ TWO-COIN VERSUS THREE-COIN ♦
MACHINES

Almost all of the slot machines found in casinos will be either two-coin machines or three-coin machines. This simply means that to win the top jackpot you must play the maximum two or three coins. You can easily determine the type of machine by looking at the payoff win display on the screen mounted over the machine. Two-coin machines will have the payoffs divided into two sections, the one on the left showing how much any winning combination of symbols will pay for a one-coin play, and the one on the right showing what these same winning combinations will pay if two coins are played per pull. On these machines the second-coin play pays double what a one-coin play would pay on the same winning combination.

Naturally, the casinos want you to play the maximum number of coins, so there is a built-in incentive for you to do so. For the top jackpot, or maybe even the top two or three jackpots, the second-coin play will pay considerably more than just double the one-coin jackpot. For instance, if the top jackpot payoff on a two-coin maximum machine is three 7's, paying, say, $1,200, the same three 7's combination will only pay $400 if you hit it with only one coin in.

Three-coin machines work on the same principle as the two-coin machines. On the payoff display, their payoff schedules are divided into three sections. The first row indicates payoffs for winning combinations hit with one coin in, the second with two coins in, and the third with the maximum of three coins in. As with the two-coin maximum machine, the three-coin maximum machine will show much higher payoffs for the top jackpots with the three-coins maximum played. Compared to two-coin machines, three-coin slot machines *look* more lucrative in their payoff structure because they show that the player will win more on any given bet. But don't be fooled! The player also has to *bet more* to get this. So while the minor pays roughly equate, in the final analysis the player will lose more money on a three-coin-maximum machine than on a two-coin machine.

Consequently, unless the machine is a progressive, stay away from three-coin slots. They will eat you up, even if it looks like you are getting paid quite a lot. You will have a much better chance of walking away with some money if you play the two-coin-maximum machines. Using only two coins per pull will leave you more money to play with, which equals more pulls on that slot, which equals more chances to get the jackpot. And it is the jackpot—*only* the jackpot—that will ever allow you to make some money at slot play.

One final piece of advice. Whatever slot you play, two-coin, three-coin, four-coin, five-coin, or whatever, *always* play the maximum number of coins. If you don't, you're shooting yourself in the foot. You will never make any money even if you win. By not playing maximum coins you deny yourself the possibility of cashing in on the top jackpot. And it doesn't matter how many smaller pays you get. Even if you get them constantly, you will *never* match the amount that one pull can get you when you hit the top jackpot with maximum coins played.

Another thing to remember is that some machines will *only* pay a jackpot, or even any number of smaller pays, if you play the maximum three coins. For instance, you will see many slot machines offering a $1,000 jackpot for three Blue 7's, with $100 for red 7's and $100 for any mixed 7's.

But these slots will *only* pay these wins if three coins are played. Although these particular machines are not that bad to play, you can go through many hundreds of dollars just for a chance at only $1,000. A good investment for a $40 tryout, but not for any serious slot play investment.

Persistent playing on such machines will end up costing you more than you can logically expect to win.

✦| ONE PAYLINE VERSUS THREE PAYLINES |✦

Most slot machines show three lines of symbols in the window, but with only the center line marked as a "payline." This means that to win anything, you must line up a winning combination on that center payline and on that line only. But many machines show three paylines: at the top, center, and bottom of the window. This means that a winning combination lined up correctly on any of the three paylines will pay. The advantage of three-payline machines is that the player has many more chances of winning and can even get double and triple pays if winning combinations appear on more than one payline together. The disadvantages are that the payoffs are usually very small, much smaller than those offered on one-payline machines, and that the top jackpot is usually paid only if you line up the proper winning symbols in the correct sequence on the bottom, or third, payline.

Three-payline machines may offer a graduated jackpot schedule, paying a smaller jackpot for winning combinations lined up on the center line, a bigger one if they are lined up on the top, or second, payline, and the highest award if they appear on the third payline.

Another disadvantage is that three-payline machines are always three-coin machines. Some machines offer five, or even eight, paylines, but this also means you have to play five or eight coins per pull. Most of the time your gaming dollar will be better spent playing two-coin maximum, three-reel, one-payline slot machines. Your money will last longer and the payoff odds—win potential relative to money invested—are much, much better than on any other kind of reel slot machine. Indeed, for the sake of further discussion, I will from now on simply omit references to any three-coin machines, any three-payline machines, any four-reel machines and any progressives.

◆ | DOUBLE-UP SYMBOLS | ◆

An increasing variety of machines now employ so-called "double up" symbols on their reels. This symbol, usually circular or in the shape of a diamond in a circle and always bearing the words "double" across its face, can be very valuable to the slot player.

The principle of this double symbol is very simple. Whenever it appears on the payline in combination with any other symbols that normally would have made a winning combination, the payoff amount is doubled. In most instances these double symbols also *substitute* for any other symbol. This means, for example, that if your machine is set to pay, say, one hundred coins for three 5's, and you get two 5's along with a double symbol on the payline, you will be paid two hundred coins, twice the regular one hundred coins. And as a further bonus, if you get *two* of the double symbols appearing on the payline with only one 5, the winning combination is quadrupled.

When choosing one of these machines, be sure not to confuse them with "Joker" machines, or "Wild Cherries," or any other machines with symbols identified on the payoff display as "wild." Wild symbols merely *substitute* for any other paying symbol; they *do not double* the payoff.

It is important, furthermore, to note that not all double-up machines are alike. Some machines, for example, will have only two double symbols—one on each of the first two reels—instead of having one on all three reels. These machines usually pay the top jackpot by combining both double symbols with a 7 on the third reel. Also, some machines will have more than one double symbol on the first reel, but only one on each of the other two.

A one-dollar, two-coin maximum, single payline slot machine employing the double symbols which also substitute for all the other symbols. This is the best kind of machine to play, in either the $1 or $5 versions.

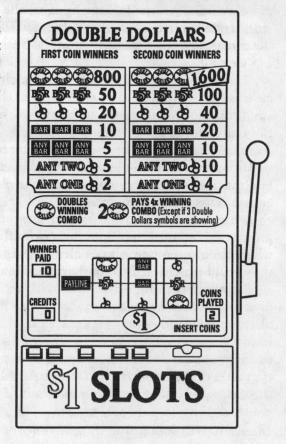

On these machines, lining up all three double symbols on the payline will generally win the top jackpot as indicated on the payoff display, but unlike the standard double-up machine, the payoffs for nonjackpot wins are *not* doubled or quadrupled.

Both of these kinds of machines are generally good to play—provided that they are machines on which the double symbols also substitute for all other symbols. On some machines that employ the double symbols the symbols *will not substitute* for other paying symbols. These machines are to be avoided. Overall, though, of all the various slot machines offered in casinos today, these will provide you with the most play, the best pays, and the best odds of hitting a top jackpot.

There are not many double-up machines available at casinos, and you will almost never find them together in a single carousel. Carousel machines are usually mixtures of the better three-coin three-paylines machines, along with some very bad ones. The good double-up machines are normally found stuck somewhere in the middle of a group of bad machines, or are relegated to some obscure part of the casino. This is not accidental. Casinos know that these machines pay better than others, so they stick one among a group of machines that does not normally pay as well and when people see one player cleaning up on the good one they will be attracted to that group of machines.

Thinking the other machines will also pay as well, they proceed to feed them their money. Likewise, by putting one of these good machines in an area of the casino not normally frequented by players, the casino will maximize profit per square foot of floor space by attracting players to that area of the casino floor. Don't be afraid to walk around the casino and look for the good kind of slot machines. If you are going to play slot machines at all, give yourself a chance to win something by applying your new knowledge toward making more informed choices. And if the casino you're in doesn't offer these kinds of slot machines, go to another. Why make this casino rich with your gaming dollar when they don't offer you the best choices or best odds?

♦ | NICKEL, QUARTER, DOLLAR, $5, $25, $100, AND $500 SLOTS | ♦

Slot machines used to take pennies, nickels, and dimes. Nowadays, you will never find a penny machine, unless it is in a museum or as a novelty attraction part of a casino promotion. You will find dime machines, but very few of them, and it would be a waste of time looking for them. Even if you do find dime machines, they are not really worth playing.

Most machines these days take nickels, quarters, dollar tokens, and $5 tokens as denominations for play. Others that take $10 tokens, $25 tokens, $100 tokens and a few that take $500 tokens are also available, but mostly in the slot VIP section of the casino. You will also find a small selection of half-dollar machines in most casinos, although the half-dollar slots you find will generally be the Video Poker machines, not reel slots.

It used to be that quarter players comprised the majority, and dollar players were prized by the casinos as among their best customers. But these days the $5 slot player is considered to be the best for the House. Consequently, an ever-increasing variety of $5 slot machines is hitting the market. These machines are mostly two-coin, three-reel, single-payline regular slots or progressive slots; some even employ the double symbols. These machines are by far the best odds machines around. You can win a lot on them, but you can also spend a lot.

If your bankroll isn't $3,000 or more, don't even think of sitting down at a $5 slot machine. Many $5 slot players will go through $3,000 to $10,000 per hour playing them, and that is not even counting the small pays they get and put back in. But you *can* be lucky. I saw a young man at Caesars Palace play just two $5 coins in a slot machine and win $18,000.00! It can happen.

But playing any slot machine can be a grind, and you must have time and money available to hold out until you get a high-paying combination. Regular $5 slot players know this and have enough money to keep playing until they get a good win. And even a relatively small pay on a $5 slot machine pays in the thousands.

Of course for the real high rollers, top casinos offer the $25, $100, and $500 slots. Needless to say, if you plan on playing any of these machines, you'd better have plenty of handy cash. It is hard to believe that anyone would actually play a $500 slot machine, but there are people who do. One of these is a Saudi prince, who plays the $500 slots in Las Vegas. Mind you, that's $500 per pull! Surrounded on all sides by armed bodyguards, the prince has an aide place the token in the machine, and then he pulls the handle. The prince has a standing credit line at Caesars Palace of $5 million.

There are in fact quite a few players like him who frequent Las Vegas. And there are many more who play the $25 and $100 machines. Even more surprising, however, is the fact that the casinos do not make most of their slot wins from these players. With the amounts of money these people gamble regularly you'd think the profit for the casino would come from them, but that is not the case.

Most of the casino's profits from slot play come from the nickel and quarter players—not even from the dollar slot players. Mostly this is because the top-dollar slot machines are, by and large, the best odds machines available. So the casino's take on these slots is lower overall, and coupled with the complimentary free food, drinks, and rooms (known as "comps"), often handed out to these players, the profit margin per machine and per player is quite low. Casinos make up for this on the quarter and nickel players, who are mainly the casual crowd and mostly have no idea of what kind of slots to play and how to play them. These players may gamble only $100 to $1,000 each per trip, as against the maybe millions of dollars for a $500 player, but there are many, many more of them. And they pump the machines full of their coins.

The nickel machines offer the worst odds under the sun, and the quarter machines are hardly better. My advice is to avoid nickel and quarter reel slots altogether, with the exception of quarter progressives and Video Keno. If you play them regardless of this advice, you'll have no fun at it and you will lose your money very fast. So if you *really* want to play nickels or quarters, play Video Poker. It will offer you better odds and better pays. And even Video Keno will give you better play and pays than any nickel or quarter reel slot machine.

If you want to play reel slots and are prepared to give it your best shot, your best bet is to play $1 or $5 machines. If you have $100 to gamble with, you'd be better off playing quarter Video Poker than quarter or nickel reel slots. If you have $1,000 to gamble with, you are far better off playing dollar reel slots than quarter reel slots. (You may even want to consider playing half-dollar or dollar Video Poker.) Dollar reel slots, $5 reel slots, and higher denominations are a good investment for your gaming dollar.

◆ | SLOT MACHINE PERCENTAGE PLAY | ◆

If you compare a modern casino with the casino of twenty years ago, you will find one striking difference: more slots and a greater variety of slots. Although the casino owners quickly recognized the value of slot players, many die-hard table players still look down at the lowly slot player. They will tell you slot machines are a poor gambling investment, that the odds against winning on slot machines are astronomical, and that percentage payouts on slots are poor. The casino's edge, they say, is too much and the randomness of slots can't be beat.

The truth is that slot machines are just like all the games of chance offered by casinos, and they are *not* as bad a game as some would make out. Casinos *do* make money from slots, but they make money from all games. And as with all games, the player can substantially improve his or her chances of winning simply by making the smart choices. One way of playing smart, as discussed in the last section, is to pay attention to the *kind* of machine you play. Another is to pay attention to the advertised payoff return—although you should keep in mind the possible fallacy of advertised percentages and not rely on this information alone.

As with Video Poker, many casinos advertise the impressive returns their slot machines offer. And, generally speaking, playing a carousel of slot machines advertised as "98 percent return" is better than playing a machine advertised as "94 percent return." But, as I said earlier, this advertising can often be a little misleading.

For example, if a casino advertises specific slot machines as "98 percent return," it *never* means that for each $1 you put into any one slot machine you will get back ninety-eight cents. A lot of first-time players make this mistake, which causes them anguish and confusion. What it *does* mean is that over the fiscal-year life cycle of that particular slot machine, it will average payoffs equivalent to 98 percent of all the money put through it.

Furthermore, even if a casino advertises "98 percent return" over a carousel of several slot machines, it does not necessarily mean that *all* the machines on the carousel are set to pay off at those rates. A few years ago one casino advertised 101 percent payback on their machines, but it only had two of those particular machines in the whole casino.

In defense of the casinos, almost all who advertise "98 percent return," or "97.4 percent payback," and so on, actually *do* have all the machines in those carousels set that way. After all, if people see other people winning, they will think this casino has good machines, and more people will come and play more machines. Nonetheless, you should be wary and aware of possible hidden truths behind catchy advertising.

My advice, then, is this: First, pick a casino that advertises a 97.4 percent or better return on slot play. This information can be found, among other places, in the local magazines that the hotels at most gambling centers supply free. Second, make sure that the payoff return applies to the specific carousel, indeed, the specific machine, you are playing on. Also, it's often a good idea to visit the casino during their busy time—early evening, after dinner, or after a show breaks—and observe the slot play. If the slot play is heavy and you see several jackpots hitting, it is a good indication that this casino is serious about slot play and offers its slot customers machines that in fact *do* pay.

Another suggestion I can offer is to play slots in the wee hours of the morning, around 2 A.M. to 8 A.M. This is a good bet for the smart slot player. Not only will you find a greater selection of machines, since most people do not by nature stay up all night, but you are more likely to pick a machine that has had extensive play the night before and perhaps is ready to pay. Many jackpots are hit in the early hours of the morning, which has a lot to do with heavy play the night before. Therefore, if you rise early or stay up late and catch the machines before the breakfast crowd gets to them, you are more likely to find a winning one.

♦| PAY CYCLES |♦

As I said before, modern slot machines are computerized and their payoffs are set by computer software programs. Still, slots do run in cycles, especially so since the winning selections are made at random by the slot machine's computer program. Although in the end the slot machine will invariably average its take and payout according to the program it is on, all slots run hot and cold from time to time. Consequently, even if you are playing one of the machines I consider good, you may hit the machine at a time when it "takes." When this happens, the machine is in the "off cycle," meaning it is making up for money paid out.

Other times you can play a bad machine and it will simply shower you with coins. That one is in a "pay cycle," meaning it has already taken in enough money and now has to pay some out. The trick is in recognizing when you are in a pay cycle and when you are not. Sounds easy, but it isn't. There is no sure way of telling how long a pay cycle will last, or how long a take cycle will last. If you play a specific slot machine for several hours, you will experience a few of these fluctuations, a give-and-take scenario.

But when you *do* hit an actual pay cycle, you'll never forget it. Suddenly it will appear that you can do no wrong. If you're lucky and hit one of these cycles, try to be smart enough to recognize it. Rake in the money, and keep a sharp eye for a downturn. A lot of machines will ease out of a pay cycle by teasing you with "almost there" pays, mostly by showing you an "almost" big jackpot. If you have played a while and racked up quite a stack of coins and the machine is still paying, keep playing it. But stop when you suddenly start to see the machine showing you these "almost" pays, especially so when it starts showing you "almost" top jackpots. When this happens, it's time to take your money and run.

This machine will eventually hit the top jackpot, as all machines eventually will, but it is quite a bit more likely to eat up the money it paid you before it does, and then it can eat up even more of your own money. Indeed, most of the time, the jackpot will hit *not* when the machine is showing you "almost" jackpots, but when it is *not* showing any "almost" combinations for the top jackpot at all. As with all gambling games, it is virtually impossible to predict when the machine will pay off, just as it is impossible to predict when the dice will roll a seven, or when the dealer will deal you a Blackjack. But if you are a percentage player, and you keep your eyes open, slot play can offer you a good opportunity for winning sizable amounts of money.

3

A SHORT HISTORY AND BACKGROUND OF TABLE GAMES

Western folklore has entrenched in the minds of generations of Americans an image of Old West gamblers and of Poker tables covered with silver dollars, money, and cards. In fact, the game played most often in the Old West was Faro. Modern Poker is actually an American invention that was first played in what used to be known as the French Territory of New Orleans around 1800; but table games, as now played in the casinos, date much farther back.

Gambling games of one type or another have been part of numerous cultures for almost as long as there have been human beings on the earth. Even in ancient cultures like Egypt people played dice games that bear a resemblance to Craps. Games like these were not in fact played on tables until fairly recently in modern history, but they nevertheless provided the basis for our current table games. Indeed, slot machines are perhaps the only gaming invention really particular to our century.

Table games are fundamentally different from the Video Poker and slot machines discussed in the preceding chapters. The biggest difference is that Video Poker and slots are solitary games. Yes, you can play them with your friends, or in groups, even in teams, but the outcome of the game you are playing depends *entirely* on you and your interaction with a machine.

With table games, on the other hand, the interaction is between you and *other people*. The dealer is a person, a human being, and not a machine. This alone makes a big difference and often intimidates novice players. Furthermore, there are often other players at the same table with you. Their way of playing and their individual approaches to the game or their interactions with the dealer can also provide a complication you don't encounter with Video Poker and slots.

Playing table games requires a greater grasp of the games themselves, and quite a bit of discipline. Unlike slots or Video Poker, "live" table games, as they are known, do not run in preset cycles. Yes, card games do run in cycles of sorts, but not in the same manner as machines. There is no program that says for every "x" number of hands, for example, the dealer will give you a Blackjack.

Table games are fully interactive, and often require a lot of decisions on the part of the player. Their rules are very specific, but within the range of these rules there is an almost infinite number of possible bets and outcomes, all the result of a combination of player's judgments, decisions, and choices, as well as the luck of the draw. The fact that there are so many different choices available to players in table games is particularly important. Although table games are played according to sometimes rigid rules, it is the player and only the player, who has the choice in how he or she will play a particular game and each hand or round of that game.

If you have ever spent a Saturday night in a friendly Poker game at home, for example, or perhaps even played

Poker in a casino environment, you are well aware of the overwhelming importance of knowledge, strategy, and choice required in such table games. And your ability to make the better choices is directly related to your knowledge of the game you are playing and the strategies with which you are familiar. Table game play therefore offers not merely the excitement of interaction between players and the House, but also a never-ending stream of mental challenges whose outcomes, and your win/loss outcome, are directly affected by the choices you make.

4
BLACKJACK

Blackjack—what a game! How simple it looks, yet how complex it truly is. Although it is also known as "21," "Pontoon," "Vingt-et-un," and "Van John," Blackjack is the popular American name given to this game, originating from the two-card combination of a black jack face value card and an ace. In its original form, Blackjack (or Vingt-et-un, translated verbatim as "twenty and one") was frequently played by such noted historical figures as Napoleon and King Louis XV of France. Vingt-et-un is still played in Monte Carlo, but its rules are now those of modern blackjack.

Around the time of World War I, a variation of the game, called Pontoon—an Australian expression still used to describe the game Down Under—was introduced by English, Australian, and New Zealand soldiers. The name Pontoon is an anglicized slang term for an incorrect pronunciation of the shortened French expression *vingt-un*, which first became *vontoon* and eventually *pontoon*. The game of Pontoon more closely resembled the rules of Blackjack as we now know it, with the exception of several variations in payoffs on specific hands—for example, three 7's was called the royal pontoon, and paid 3:1.

Although there appears to be no documented historical proof that the game of Pontoon was brought to America by returning World War I veterans, it is quite likely that this was the case; the game then underwent its Americanization and eventually evolved into the Blackjack game we know today.

◆ | HOW TO RECOGNIZE BLACKJACK | ◆

In the modern casino, Blackjack is played on a semicircular table, with the round "half-moon" portion of the table facing the players, and the straight edge side of the table facing the dealer. Dealers stand in an area called the "pit," and a Blackjack pit will have several Blackjack tables arranged together around the center space. The Blackjack tables are covered with felt, and the player's side of the table also has a comfortable rim of padding where the players may rest their arms. Most Blackjack tables will accommodate seven players, each player occupying one "spot" on the table.

These spots are usually identified by a circle painted on the felt in front of where the player would sit down. Chairs are provided for the players, and one chair is placed in front of each of these painted spots. The spot is the area into which the player will place his or her gaming chips, or cash, indicating that a bet is being made on the next hand.

The spots are not necessarily in the shape of a circle. They can be semicircles, or just the logo of the casino you are in. But all spots are clearly marked in front of the player's area and a bet can be placed only in this area. The dealers will be quick to point this out to a player in case he places his money outside, or even partly outside, that area.

With the rounded side facing the player, about halfway between the player and the dealer is a painted semicircle on which are written some of the basic rules of play at that particular table in that particular casino.

Every Blackjack table will have the words "Insurance pays 2 to 1" written in that area (for explanation see point 10 in the section on Simple Strategy). Right behind this is another crucial piece of information the player should always pay attention to. These are either the words, "Dealer must hit soft 17," or, "Dealer must stand on all 17." The difference is very important and we will explore it shortly.

Immediately in front of the dealer is a tray mounted on the top of the Blackjack table. In this tray is the House "bank" for this table, which contains many gaming chips of different denominations.

Almost all table games are now played with gaming chips and not cash. It is from this tray that the dealer will

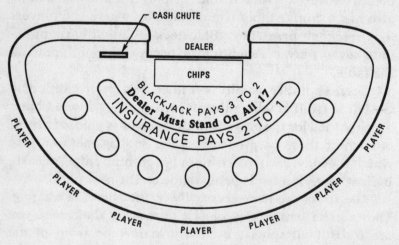

A typical Blackjack table.

give the player "change" in gaming chips when he sits down to play. From this tray the dealer will pay winners, and into this tray the dealer will place losing bets.

A running count of the amount of money in this tray is often made by the casino Pit Boss, the "manager" of that Blackjack pit for that shift. This is done so that the House can get a progressive tally of how the game is doing, whether this table is winning for the House or not, and also to make sure that table always has enough chips of every denomination to allow for uninterrupted play.

The "cash chute" is to the right of the dealer, the player's left, and consists of a small slit in the top of the table underneath of which is a secure box. When a player sits at a Blackjack table, or any table game, and places cash money in front of him for conversion to gaming chips—i.e., asks for "change"—the dealer will take the money, count it, convert it into gaming chips, and then stuff the cash bills into this little slot. The money falls down into the box, called the "drop box"; the money in the drop box is what is called "the drop."

◆| HOW TO PLAY |◆

The object of the game of Blackjack—in which you are first dealt two cards and subsequently permitted to draw more—is to put together a hand whose card values, when added together, will total 21, or as close as possible to 21 without going over. At the same time, of course, the object is to win; and to do this the value of your cards must be higher than those retained by the dealer. There are many different ways of dealing Blackjack and many rules particular to the casino you are in that determine which game is best. In this book I will only deal with simple strategy, as it affects the player, and an overview of Blackjack play in general.

In Blackjack all cards are counted at their face value, with the exception of the ace. Simply put, cards whose printed numerical value is 2 through 10 are counted as having precisely that value. Therefore, if you are dealt one 2-value card, one 8-value card and one 9-value card, your total is 19. Face cards—jacks, queens, and kings—are counted as having a value of 10. Therefore if you are dealt one queen and one 8-value card, the total value of your hand is 18. The ace card is different. This card can have, at your discretion, a value of either 1 or 11.

The best possible hand in Blackjack is a combination of an ace with a 10-value or face card. This is an automatic 21, when counting the ace as an 11, and is called Blackjack, or a "natural." It cannot be beaten, unless the dealer also has the same combination, in which case the hand is a "push," a tie.

When you first approach a table you have the choice of sitting in any available seat. If the game is already in progress, with other players present, sit at any open seat of your liking. When the hand they are currently playing is over, you can ask for "change" and push your money toward the dealer. However, be careful not to place the money in the bet spot in front of you. If you do this, chances are the dealer will assume you are making a cash bet, known as "money plays," and will deal you cards before you have a chance to ask for change. If this happens, you are stuck, and all the money you placed on the table will play on the hand you are dealt.

After you have asked for change, the dealer will give you an assortment of gaming chips with which to play. Depending on the amount of currency you are changing, dealers will mostly anticipate the kind of bets you will make and give you gaming chips accordingly. But you can ask the dealer for any combination of gaming chips you like.

After you are given change, you select the amount you wish to bet on the next hand. This has to be at least the minimum bet amount for that table and can be up to the maximum bet amount for that table. The maximum and minimum betting limits are displayed on a sign, usually at the dealer's left, player's right, and normally it will say something like: "Minimum $5 Maximum $500." These limits vary from table to table, and from casino to casino. Simply put, this tells you what level of game this table is set up to play. If all you want to play are small bets, say, $1 to $5 per hand, don't sit at a table whose sign indicates limits higher than that. You could get caught in a game whose stakes are higher than you can afford.

After you have received your gaming chips in exchange for currency, place the chips you wish to bet on the next hand in the spot in front of you, and the dealer will deal the next hand. All cards are dealt left to right of the dealer, player's right to left. You will receive your cards in turn with the other players on the table, depending on your position at the table.

The first position at the Blackjack table is called "First Base," and it is the seat immediately to the dealer's left. It is so called because the player sitting in that position will always get the first card out.

The opposite side of the table, at the far end and dealer's right, is called "Third Base," because the player sitting in this position will always get the last card dealt to players in the round of dealing, and the one just before the card that the dealer deals to himself. The Third Base position at the Blackjack table is important because the player in that position controls, to some degree, which cards the dealer will receive in the event that the dealer must draw more cards. The Third Base player's decisions in how he plays his hand can, therefore, determine if the rest of the players at the table, including himself, will win or lose.

For example, if the Third Base player has been dealt, say, 16 on the first two cards and the dealer is showing a 6 as his up card, chances are that the dealer has a draw to a bust hand, often having a 10-value card as the down card. This means that any further card he draws higher than a 5 will bust him, thereby making every player's hand at that table a winner. The card that the dealer will deal himself is *exactly* the same card that the player at Third Base will draw in this case if he asks for a hit. So, if that Third Base player had the 16 and asked for a hit and received, say, a 10, he busts. He has lost, but now the dealer has a chance to draw the second card in the deck in sequence and that card may very well be a 5.

Consequently, if the dealer did have a 6 as his up card and a 10 as his down card, that other 10-value card the Third Base player drew would have busted the dealer's hand. But because the Third Base player was a bad player, the dealer has now made 21 and, more than likely, won all player bets at the whole table. It is for these reasons that bad decisions by a player at Third Base can make the dealer a good hand even if he started with a bad hand; conversely, smart play at Third Base can often result in a dealer's bust hand, providing the whole table with a win. In addition, the player at Third Base will also get to see all the cards played by the players before him in turn, which can assist in strategy play and card counting (to be discussed shortly). For these reasons frequent Blackjack players prefer the Third Base position.

If you approach a table where there are no players, you can sit at any seat. Don't be afraid of sitting at a table where there are no players. Many players make this mistake and often try to crowd into a Blackjack game already in progress. Safety in numbers may be good for other games, such as Craps, but not for Blackjack. A one-on-one game with the dealer offers the best odds you can hope for in this game. Casual players are often intimidated by the prospect of sitting at an empty Blackjack table. Don't be.

If you are new at the game, just tell the dealer and he or she will help you. After all, it is easier for the dealer to help a novice player when there are no other players at the game, than if the table is full and explanations are distractions to both the dealer and the other players.

When you approach a new game, as an empty table is called, the first thing you will probably hear the dealer say is: "Shuffle." Dealers say this to let the Pit Boss know that a player has sat down at this game and that a new shuffle is about to begin. After the cards are shuffled, the dealer will ask you to cut the cards. For this you will be offered a colored piece of plastic the same size as the playing cards. These "cut cards" are just plain pieces of plastic cut in the same shape as the rest of the cards so they fit in the deck. Mostly they are red in color, but they can be yellow, or any other color. They are used only for three purposes: one, to cut the deck; two, to place within the freshly cut deck to indicate the next shuffle point; and three, to place at the bottom of the deck so there is no possibility of dealing cards from the bottom. To "cut" the deck means to place this colored cut card somewhere in the deck, after which the dealer moves the stack of cards above the cut card to the bottom of the deck.

He then "burns" (sets aside) the top card, places the colored cut card into the deck about one-third of the way from the bottom, places an extra colored cut card at the bottom of the deck, and begins the game. During the course of the game the dealer will eventually reach the cut card he has placed in the deck. At this point the cards now dealt will be the last hand before the next shuffle.

The point of "burning" the top card is to avoid so-called "funny shuffles," or cheating, and to take that card out of play in case some players have caught a glimpse of it. Some casinos in fact burn several cards, all dealt face down in front of the dealer for that reason and then placed into the discard tray, where all exposed cards are placed after each hand. When Blackjack games were still being dealt first-card-to-the-last, card counters took advantage of knowing which cards were left, so this rule, and others like it, were introduced to combat this player advantage. But in the current way of dealing Blackjack this burn card, or cards, have little effect, especially so to the casual player. In addition, many casinos are now employing the services of a diabolical monster machine called the Shuffle Master. This machine shuffles a single deck of cards and is supposed to speed up play. Many casinos now use it in Blackjack, as well as some new table game variations like Progressive Caribbean Stud Poker, and other game innovations.

My experience has been that instead of speeding up the game, this Shuffle Master machine slows it down to a crawl. But speeding up the game is not the primary reason casinos like to employ it. It is yet another attempt to get the human element out of table games. Live dealers can make mistakes; robots cannot. And live dealers often shuffle the cards in the same manner, perhaps unknowingly to the player's advantage. The House wouldn't object so much if the erratic shuffles of a live dealer were always in the House favor. But live dealers are just that, live human beings, and therefore their shuffling action cannot be controlled. And, especially in high-stakes games, just one shuffle that would pay the player a large payoff can hurt the House enormously.

So the powers that be have created this monstrosity to eliminate such possibilities. But machines too are fallible, and this one is especially so. Not only does it not shuffle the deck properly, it delays the game and further dehumanizes a game already polluted by overregulation and a proliferation of unfavorable rules. I certainly hope that players will become sophisticated enough to avoid tables using this machine.

♦ | TO "DOUBLE DOWN" AND "SPLIT" | ♦

To "double down" means to double your bet and receive one more card only. This is another choice that you can make, and it offers you additional advantages to win and win more. All casinos will allow you to double down on any first two cards dealt, regardless of their combined value and regardless of whether they are of matching value—a necessary requirement for splitting. If you want to double down, you place the cards face up in front of the betting circle, on the dealer's side, and place a bet equal to your original bet next to it. You should always say, "Double down," when you do this. This is especially important in case you also have an option to split—such as with two 5's—but want to double down instead. If you do not say it, dealers may assume you want to split, or vice versa. If you want to split cards, you should say, "Split." Most casinos, however, have special rules with regard to splitting cards.

In all casinos players are always allowed to split the first two cards, as long as these cards have the same value. By splitting, players in effect play two hands, and have to place a bet equal to the original bet on each of the two hands now in action.

Each hand is then played in the same manner as any single hand would have been. The hand to the player's right is decided first, win or lose, and then the second hand is played independently in the same way. If, however, you split two cards, say, two 9's, and then are dealt another 9 to one or both of your hands, often a casino will not permit you to split them again. And a few casinos—even when they permit splitting and resplitting—may not allow you to re-split aces.

All casinos will allow you to *split* aces, but if you do, you will only be dealt *one* additional card on each of the two aces. This also applies to casinos that permit you to resplit aces—you will always get only one more card on each of the split or resplit aces. Normally, if you split, say, two 9's, and received a 3 on the first hand, you can still hit the hand and get another card, or as many cards as you want to ask for, until you make 21, bust, or choose to stand. And if you get, say, another 9, you can split it again, and again if another 9 is dealt, and so on up till all the 9-value cards are out, if they were so grouped together in the shuffle. But when you are splitting aces, you must always remember that, no matter what the extra card dealt on each split ace is, you *cannot* ask for a hit and draw yet another card.

The *only* exception to this is in those casinos which will allow you to resplit aces in the event that one or both second cards dealt to you over the first two split aces is also another ace. Thereafter the same rules apply, and you can only get one extra card over each of the resplit aces.

◆ | SINGLE DECK, TWO DECKS, AND SIX-DECK SHOE | ◆

Most Blackjack games are dealt either as "single deck," "two decks," or "six-deck shoe." Single deck means one deck of fifty-two cards, no joker or wild cards. Two decks are just that, and a six-deck shoe is a box that looks like a shoe from which the dealer deals the cards to the players. This shoe has six 52-card decks in it, all shuffled together. The strategy of Blackjack play is different for each of these situations and is complicated as well by other factors inherent in the casino rules, the number of players at the table, the position at which you are sitting, and so on.

The single deck was commonly used in Blackjack games until the 1960s. However, smart players quickly developed several card-counting strategies, which gave them a big edge over the House. Counting cards is not very difficult with a single deck.

In a single deck there are four of everything—four aces, four kings, four queens, and so on. As the cards are dealt, it is quite easy to remember how many aces have been dealt, how many 10-value cards, how many 5-value cards, and so on. Therefore the observant players were able to determine which cards were left and bet accordingly—meaning they made bigger bets when they knew there were more 10-value cards left in the deck than 2-, 3-, 4-, 5-, and 6-value cards, and bet less when the count was reversed.

This took most of the risk out of their betting. Card counting is not illegal, but skilled card counters made the casinos uneasy. The casinos finally put a stop to it by altering the rules. Over the years such various changes to the rules of casino play have made Blackjack a pretty hard game to beat, even for a very skilled card-counting player.

The first changes were to stop dealing single decks from top to bottom, and introducing the burn and cut cards to reduce the number of cards played from the deck. Card counting thus became less accurate. As card counting and betting systems improved, casinos simply went to more decks, from one deck to two, to four, to six, and even to eight decks in some places. This makes it virtually impossible to get a true count.

The by-product of these changes, however, was that Blackjack became much less popular than it had been. And, with the advent of Video Poker and more sophisticated slot machines, modern casinos soon began to feel the pinch. So they started to reduce the number of decks and somewhat liberalize the rules all over again—although, realistically, these changes were more cosmetic than real. Even today many casinos tout single-deck Blackjack games. But when you go to play there, you soon find out that on a full table a dealer will average a mere two hands per deck before shuffling. Even if you get a one-on-one game—difficult to find at best but mostly available around 3 A.M.—you soon discover that casino rules will force the cut card to be placed about halfway through the deck. This means only half the cards will be dealt before a shuffle, and even with a one-on-one game between player and dealer, the player can expect at best three or four hands. In addition, many casinos will simply have the dealer shuffle the deck each hand, or after every two hands, if they even think you are making educated bets.

The point is, a single-deck Blackjack game is theoretically the best to play, but in reality no casino will give you an opportunity to play it using all available player advantages. Standard Blackjack games are now mostly of the two-deck hand-dealt and the six-deck-shoe variety.

In most casinos offering two-deck games (two decks shuffled together), the cut card will be placed about one-third of the way from the bottom, so the player will see many more cards dealt. In a two-deck game, there are eight of everything, instead of four. This is probably the best game to play if you have any inclination to practice any sort of card-counting and betting strategies.

A six-deck game will use six of the standard decks of cards, dealt from the shoe. Different casinos have their own policies as to where the cut card must be placed, although most will place it halfway, so in reality the player will see only three decks dealt. In a six-deck game there are twenty-four of everything, and it is almost impossible to practice accurate card counting. The advantage to the player, however, is that cards tend to group in the six-deck shoe, and therefore it is possible to hit winning streaks more often than with two-deck, or certainly single-deck games.

Current casino rules of shuffling, cut card placements, number of burn cards discarded prior to play, hitting "soft 17" and, lately, using shuffling machines instead of dealers, all make the game so much more difficult to beat that any strategy, even professional card-counting strategy, is rendered almost worthless.

What strategies can still be applied require such a level of knowledge, expertise, experience, mental skill, concentration, dedication, length of play, and bankroll, that almost all casual players should leave this field to the very few pros who are still able to eke out a living at Blackjack play.

◆| SOFT AND HARD |◆

In Blackjack a "soft hand" means a combination, on the first two cards dealt, of an ace with any card *other than* any 10-value card, and is so called because the player can count the ace as either 11 or as 1. For instance, if you are dealt an ace and a 3-value card, you have a "soft hand"—your hand can be either 14 or 4, depending on how you choose to tally the cards. This is called a "soft 14."

The importance of a soft hand is that it gives the player the option of taking a hit without any danger of going over 21 and busting. It offers the player a risk-free chance to get closer to 21, and closer to a winning hand, which is especially useful if the dealer's up card suggests he might have a hand better than the one so far dealt to the player.

In our example, the player can count the ace and 3 together as 4, and receive a hit of 10, for a total of 14.

Although it is not a good hand—indeed, it has the same total value as if the player had counted the ace as 11, it nonetheless offers the player one more chance to draw another card. The player may then draw a 6-value card, giving him a final value of 20 for that hand. If the player's hand had not been a soft hand, if it had instead constituted of a 10-value card and a 4-value card (so-called "hard 14," also known as a "stiff"), the first hit of 10 would have put him over 21 for a bust. In effect, since he is able to use the ace as a 1, the player with the soft hand can give himself two or more additional chances to win. Many times the player can substantially improve a bad hand by doing this. In fact, a soft hand will sometimes allow you to get close to 21, or indeed make 21, by drawing six or more cards. This is called "six and over," and in some casinos it is an automatic winner, often paying a bonus 2:1.

Soft hands are so important that many casinos will try to eliminate the player's edge these hands provide by altering the rules of play; such altered Blackjack rules will now require that dealers in these casinos "hit soft 17."

The number 17 is crucial in Blackjack because it can be either the worst hand for the player (you can't hit it because any card other than an ace, 2, 3, or 4 will bust you) or the dealer (who has to, by casino rules, stand on hard 17), or the best of a bad hand for the player; because any 17 is basically a get-nowhere hand, it is the best of the bad lot if you're lucky enough to push with it or win on it if the dealer busts. As in Craps, where the number 7 can be either the player's friend or foe, so in Blackjack the number 17 can make or break the player's hand.

Many casinos offer Blackjack games where the House rules, painted on the felt covering of the Blackjack table, indicate: "Dealer must stand on all 17." These are favorable rules for the player, and mean that even if the dealer gets an ace with a 6, a soft 17 hand, he *must* count the ace as 11, and therefore the total hand as 17. This means that the dealer will have *no* options, and must play this hand as if it had been a hard 17, that is, play it in the same manner as if it were a 7-value card with a 10-value card—a *hard* 17. If, on the other hand, the dealer "must hit soft 17," that casino allows their dealers to take more cards and therefore offers more chances for the dealer to make a good hand.

If, for example, you have a hard 17, and the dealer turns up an ace and a 6—a soft 17—in the casinos where "dealer must stand on *all* 17" you would have an automatic push— a good result for this hand. But in the casinos where the dealer must hit soft 17, this is not the case. Many times the dealer will make a better hand than he had, and your automatic push now turns into a more frequent loser. And the same applies to any other hand you may have, even those considerably better than just a hard 17. As a result, if you are playing in a casino which clearly states that "Dealer must hit soft 17," you are giving up part of your edge, a portion of your choices, and therefore are not playing a game as favorable to you as those you can easily find in other casinos.

♦| RULES TO WATCH OUT FOR |♦

In addition to the 17 hands, you will be wise to find out whether the casino you are at places other restrictions on Blackjack. Some casinos, for example, will only allow you to double down if the combined value of the first two cards dealt is 10 or 11. This means that if the dealer is showing, say, a 6 as the up card—normally a good time for you to double down because it indicates a possible bad hand for the dealer—and you have a first-two-card total of 9, you cannot double down, even though this would generally be a good time to do it.

By eliminating this choice on all two-card values except 10 and 11, the casino further reduces your choices, and hence your ability to win money. It is a good idea to stay away from casinos with these restrictions. These days it is quite hard to find a casino that offers all the favorable options for Blackjack play, since most will allow only some of the better options. If you do find a casino that offers all of them, chances are they will only be offered on the six-deck-shoe game. Still, these are the games to look for.

♦| SIMPLE STRATEGY |♦

Strategy of play for Blackjack involves a set of playing rules called "Basic Strategy," and a much more involved and complicated series of disciplines called "Advanced Basic Strategy" and "Advanced Card Counting Strategy."

Basic Strategy is a set of rules a player can easily memorize that dictate which hands the player should stand on, hit, double down, or split, always taking into consideration the value of the dealer's up card. This Basic Strategy is very important to any player of Blackjack because it offers an easy-to-remember guide to the decisions that yield the best possible result in the player's favor.

Much of this strategy and casino rules of play are based on the notion that in any deck of cards there are more 10-value cards than all the others—10's, jacks, queens, and kings combined as 10-value cards, versus any of the other cards, treated individually, in a singles deck of 52 cards.

However, Basic Strategy is not infallible. Since you don't see what the dealer's down card is, and don't know what the other cards in the deck are, there is still a fair element of luck and guesswork involved. But Basic Strategy, when properly played, can substantially affect the game's House edge and provide the player with a real and effective framework on which to base his decisions.

When Basic Strategy is used by the player in combination with applied advanced card counting, money management and betting progression strategies, then Blackjack can yield an actual player advantage, entirely eliminating the House edge. But this advantage is small, rendered almost useless by various unfavorable House rules (like those discussed above), and offers little satisfaction to the casual player.

Details on Basic Strategy and the more advanced disciplines are readily available in many books specifically on Blackjack, and I would highly recommend that you read one if you are interested in a very detailed analysis of the game. For most gamblers, however, this is more information than you'll need. For practical purposes, then, I offer some simple guidelines which should help in your decision making:

1. If the dealer is showing a 7 card or higher, and you have a two-card total of 12, 13, 14, 15, or 16, always take a hit and continue to hit your hand until you get 17 or better. Any of these hands (12, 13, 14, 15, or 16) is an automatic loser if the dealer has a 7 or higher showing and 10 hiding. You risk little by taking a hit, assuming the dealer already has beaten your hand. To improve your hand is your only option. This is especially true when you hold a soft hand. In this case you take no risk at all and have a terrific chance to make a winning hand out of a bad one.

2. If the dealer shows an up card of 2, 3, 4, 5, or 6, stand on any hand that is 12 and over, hit any hand that is 8 or less, and double down on everything else. This is especially true if the dealer has a 5 or a 6 showing.

     These are the worst dealer hands possible, since for the most part the dealer will get a 15 or 16 and will have to take another card. This makes it likely he will bust. And if you have a soft hand, even soft 17, double down. You are now playing *both* that you will improve the hand you already have, *and* that the dealer will bust. These circumstances are the best possible options for the player to make money.

3. Never hit a hard 17 or higher. If you are dealt a hard 17, stand, no matter what. Any card higher than a 4 will bust you out, so your chances are better to stay and see what the dealer turns up. The dealer may show a 10 but be hiding a 6, then draw a 6 and bust out. If you hit your hard 17, that 6, as next card out, would have busted you and you would have lost. This way you win. Whatever the dealer is showing, if you have 17, 18, 19, or 20 on the first two cards, stand. Of course, if you have 21, a Blackjack, you win anyway, so why hit it? As strange as it sounds, people do make silly plays like this.

4. Always split aces. When given two aces as your first two cards, you have either a total of 2 or a total of 12, both bad hands. But if you split the aces, and get 10 on each, you have two hands of 21, both winners (unless the dealer also makes 21 in which case your hands are a push, or the dealer has Blackjack, in which case only your original bet will lose). These two-ace hands are *not* Blackjacks, a common misconception among casual players. Remember, after you split the aces, they automatically count as 11 each, and you only get one more card on each of the two hands. If you are dealt another ace on either or both hands, and you are at a casino that allows you to resplit aces, split them again. Whatever the case, and whatever the dealer is showing as his up card, splitting aces will give you a much better chance of winning than if you simply counted the hand as 2 or 12 and continued hitting.

5. Always split two 8's. No matter what the dealer has, even if he is showing an ace, split the 8's. Two 8's make 16, the worst hand in Blackjack. By splitting the two 8's, you stand a better chance of making at least one hand a winner, thereby saving your money. If one hand wins but the other loses, one hand pays the other, so you have lost nothing. But if you didn't split the 8's, chances are you would have busted out on the 16 and lost it all. And if you draw a 10 to both hands, you have two 18's and have made two decent hands out of one bad one.

6. Never split two 10-value cards. This hand is a total of 20, a very good one. The object in Blackjack is to achieve 21, but if you have 20 on the first two cards dealt to you there is only one hand that the dealer can beat you with, and that is 21. If the dealer has 20 as well, you push and don't lose. Any other combination for the dealer means an automatic winner

for you. Many times I see players splitting two 10-value cards and winding up losing all their money and at the same time incurring the wrath of all the other players at the table. Doing this can easily mess up the favorable order, or count, of the cards yet to be dealt and is financial suicide.

7. Never split two 5's. Two 5's equal 10, so double down instead and ask for "one card only, please." If you split the two 5's and get two 10's, you make two bad hands out of a good hand. It's already hard enough to win, so when you have a chance to win twice your initial bet, take it and don't play foolishly.

8. Always double down on 11. Any first two cards dealt to you equaling 11 offer the best chance you have to make 21 with just one more card, or at least a great hand with almost any other card. Also, you cannot bust out, making this double-down bet even better. This is also an edge you have over the House. By doubling down you are taking full advantage of the favorable odds offered to you.

9. Always double down on 10, unless the dealer is showing a 10-card up or an ace. The principle here is the same as for doubling down on 11, and works in the player's favor to nearly the same extent.

10. Never take insurance, unless you also hold a Blackjack. Insurance is a sucker bet, and is offered as a means of making the player bet on whether or not the dealer has a Blackjack when he has an ace showing as the up card. Most of the time the dealer does not have a Blackjack, and it will cost you an additional 50 percent of your bet to find out. If the dealer does not have a Blackjack, you lose the additional 50 percent bet you made and then stand a good chance of losing your original bet.

If the dealer does have a Blackjack, tough luck. Swallow the loss and play the next hand. You won't win every hand you play, but the extra 50 percent bet isn't worth spending on the off chance the dealer does in fact have a Blackjack. The situation is different only if you are holding Blackjack yourself. In that case, ask for "even money." This means the dealer will pay you even money (as opposed to 3 to 2) even before he looks to see if he also has a Blackjack. If he does, you would have pushed and not won anything, so by asking for even money you made yourself a winner out of a no-contest hand. If the dealer does not have the Blackjack, you still win the even money, and it is better to win 100 percent of your money than risk no win in order to win that extra 50 percent.

In addition to these simple guidelines, there are many more specific suggestions that could be made depending on the values of a player's first two cards and the dealer's up card. They can be found in the books on Blackjack strategy, and if listed here would result in a whole book on just that subject alone.

What I have offered here are the most basic suggestions for strategy play in Blackjack. Even if you have no further interest in reading about Blackjack and Blackjack strategy, the simple strategy I have outlined will help make you a smarter player and give you a better chance of making your vacation gaming dollar count for more in your Blackjack play.

I should point out, however, that some players are plainly lucky and can win regardless of how badly they play. Such big streaks of blind luck are very rare, but they do happen. Why they happen is a quirk of nature or perhaps a favored light of God upon that lucky player. If you *do* recognize that you are having one such lucky streak, you will quickly find out that you can seemingly do no wrong; in that case there is no reason why you shouldn't press your luck to the limit. How you recognize such streaks is an art particular only to you, but if it happens to you, go for it.

Throughout this chapter on Blackjack, I emphasized that smart play will provide you with financial longevity. Nonetheless, luck still plays an important element. This is true of all gambling games—it would not be gambling without such an element of chance. Luck can be both good and bad. If you have good luck, it is important to recognize it and maximize on it. It is likewise important to know when it's over.

Knowing when to quit sounds easy. In practice, especially in a casino environment, it is one of the hardest decisions you will ever have to make. To illustrate this point, I offer stories of two people with diametrically opposite results. These are true stories.

First, the story of a Blackjack dealer from the Sands in Las Vegas. I was playing at his table one night and we struck up a conversation. The way it began was a long winning streak for me. I had made twelve winners in a row, pressing my bets, and was accumulating a nice stack of chips. Naturally I was happy. But the dealer looked at me, smiled, and told me his story.

It seems this dealer was also an avid Blackjack player, and the night before he had gone to the Santa Fe Casino, a homey place on the north I-95 outside of Las Vegas on the way to Reno. This is a fairly new casino and caters primarily to locals and road travelers. That night my dealer friend had gone there with $100 to play Blackjack. He proceeded to win several hands and had made quite a sum of money. What differentiated this player from other players was that he practiced the "play with their money" principle. Simply put, this means that after he had achieved more winnings than the $100 he had brought with him, he pocketed the original $100 and from then on played with the House money—their money.

This is a very wise approach, because now you risk none of your own money and continually give yourself an ever-increasing chance to win a lot by using the won money. If you treat this won money as your stake, with no feelings of personal possession, you eliminate the fear of losing what is yours. In essence, this means you are no longer playing with "scared" money. Therefore it becomes psychologically easier to bet large amounts that you would normally not even think of betting if you were risking your own hard-earned cash.

This dealer had reached such a point. Now he was pressing his bets to higher and higher amounts, and soon reached the table maximum of $200 per hand, per spot. He was still winning, so he played two spots. He continued to win and began to bet three spots, then four, and finally all seven spots with table maximum. It was at this point that one of those unfathomable lucky streaks hit him, and he knew it. He was able to recognize it and played into it.

When God is smiling at you like this, you can do no wrong. Neither could our dealer friend at this time. All the rules of play went out the window. He split 10's and 5's, doubled on stiffs, everything contrary to all the rules of play. But the clincher was: just at this particular time, his dealer proceeded to bust out twenty-seven consecutive hands.

This is the kind of story that sends shivers up my spine. This man wound up leaving the table with $28,000, from an original investment of $100. The good part of this story is that he also knew when to leave. But he nonetheless lamented that if the table had had a higher maximum bet he would have made tons more money. Still, he was a truly happy camper.

At this point I must warn you again against trying to press your luck when all you have is a chance for some skilled play. Of all the times you go to play Blackjack, or any casino game, 99 percent of the time the *only* chance you will have to win some money is to play it smart. And, on that rare occasion when you do hit a lucky streak like the one I just described, *if* you're smart enough to see it, and you play it smart, count your lucky stars and your money, take it and run, and don't think you'll ever do it again. Here's the second story to make this point.

A few years ago there was a cocktail waitress at the Stardust Hotel and Casino in Las Vegas who worked hard all night, serving drinks and hustling tips. At the end of the night she could reasonably expect two to three hundred dollars in tips, over and above her minimum-wage salary. One night after work she stopped by the Sands and started to play Blackjack.

Like my dealer friend in the above story, she also hit a mammoth winning streak and could do no wrong. For twenty hours she sat there winning constantly. By that time she had the table covered with $100 chips, a total of some $200,000. Her friends came and told her to go home, quit, retire, buy a house, anything. Even the dealers at the Sands told her so, and even the management. They were happy for her. They all know how hard work is and how uncommon a winning streak like this is. But to no avail.

Unlike my dealer friend at the Santa Fe, this young woman didn't know when to quit. Over the next twelve hours she lost it all, then lost her $300 stake, then lost $1,000 in credit, then $500 of borrowed money, and by that evening was back at her job running cocktails for customers.

There is a reason why I'm giving both sides of these win/ loss stories. Every gambling establishment will tell you, "Bet with your head, not over it." It is good advice. Most people think that casinos don't want you to win. They do. They know that losers will greatly outnumber the winners, and that a big winner is the best publicity they can get, the kind advertising money can't buy.

But if you are going to be reckless about your play, like the cocktail waitress, they'll give up trying to help you and instead cater to your silliness. After all, the casino industry is a hospitality industry, and if the customer insists on being stupid, a good hospitality business will bite the bullet and cater to that customer and take his money.

Curious as it may seem, some people get more enjoyment out of losing than winning. I know of a foreign gambler at Caesars Palace who comes to town twice a year, plays high-end slots, spends a lot of money, and is never happy if he wins. He always says: "I lost, but that's the way it should be." Wrong! For him, that may be the case. But the purpose of my book is to convince you that losing is *not* the natural outcome of gambling, and that if you play smart, you can win.

So don't be afraid to win, and you may find yourself in the situation my dealer friend did at the Santa Fe. And if you don't, but try to play silly, not smart, chances are very good that you'll wind up like the cocktail waitress from the Stardust.

5
CRAPS

♥ ♦ ♣ ♠

Although the game of Craps is now experiencing a resurgence in the modern casino, much like table games in general, the sad fact of recent history is that it almost became a dead art. If you look at movies from the 1930s and especially the 1940s, you can see kids shooting a hot game of Craps in the basement of the reformatory or back alley, or soldiers in World War II enjoying the freedom and excitement of a "pass" roll. But to the two post–World War II generations, weaned on mechanical toys and games, the Craps game was virtually unknown. This too is changing.

My first experience with the game of Craps was in two movies. One was a comedy film with Dean Martin and Jerry Lewis, where they wind up in Las Vegas, broke, and turn a dime into $8,000 at the Craps table. The other was a film with Rock Hudson, where he played the owner of the Tropicana Hotel and had to come up with several million dollars fast in order to save his resort. He did it by going across the street to the competition (only possible in movies), and winning millions at the Craps table by making something like twenty-one consecutive passes. There are even more contemporary and factual stories of famed Craps wins and winners, like the Las Vegas man who started with $100 and parlayed it into $1.5 million! Of course, he lost a million the next day, but he still had $500,000 left.

Craps does not look as simple as Blackjack. It has a huge variety of betting options, and many casual players can easily find themselves confused. And since Craps players are notoriously noisy, yelling and screaming a lot, and calling for strange things like "double odds," "box cars," "horn," "high-lo," "all across," "press it," "hard ways," and other seemingly alien terms, Craps can appear to be an intimidating game. But the truth is that Craps is the kind of game that can be as complicated, or as simple, as you want it to be. If you want to take full advantage of all the betting options offered, there is a lot to learn. But there is plenty of fun, excitement, and profit to be had at the Craps table with just a simple minimum of solid information.

•| HOW TO RECOGNIZE CRAPS |•

Craps is a dice game played inside a large sunken table not unlike a bathtub, on which is painted a rather complicated-looking layout. Along the rim at the top of the table are two rows of grooves, called the "rail," and it is there that players stash their chips. These tables are easily spotted in the casino not only because they look so odd compared to the other table games, but also because a Craps game is almost always in progress somewhere in the casino and more often than not is accompanied by loud yells, cheers, and jeers from its players.

Four people work the game. The man in the suit, usually sitting behind the table on the pit side and in front of the

SHORT END

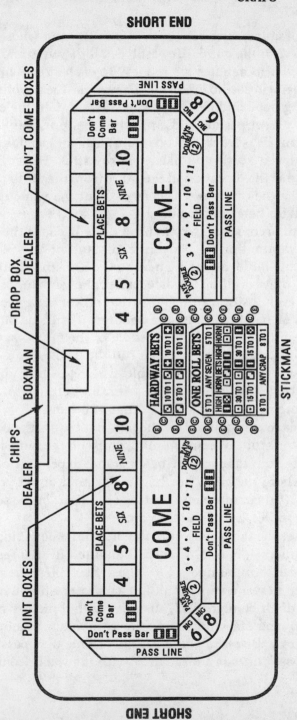

A standard Craps table layout.

SHORT END

stacks of chips, is the Boxman. He is the one whose decisions govern the game. He resolves all disputes and questions and also handles the money. To each side of him are the dealers, in casino uniforms. They make the payoffs, pick up losing bets, and generally run the game. In the center, on the player's side and opposite the Boxman, is the Stickman. He is a dealer, also in uniform, and wields a long stick, curved at the end like a hockey stick. He is the one who moves the dice around the table from player to player. He is also the one you will hear call out the value of each roll, call for bets, and so on.

There are no seats around the table because the game is played standing up. Players can stand at any position around the table, including next to the Stickman and dealers. The player rolling the dice, called the "shooter," stands at whatever position at the table that player occupies when it is his or her turn to be the shooter. If it turns out that player stands exactly in the middle of the table—say next to the Stickman—he or she can roll the dice toward either of the two short ends of the table, as long as both dice hit the farthest side wall of the Craps table relative to where the shooter happens to be standing at the time.

The layout is painted on the felt that covers the bottom of this "bathtub." Placing gaming chips on the table layout indicates both that you are betting and, depending on precisely where the chips are laid, what kind of bet you are making. (I'll get more into betting situations in the section on How to Bet, a little further on.)

Across the table, closest to the pit (the dealer's side), are the numbers 4, 5, 6, 8, 9, and 10, painted in squares, and called the "box numbers." To the left of these numbers, from the player's vantage point, is another box with the words "don't come bar 12," usually with a picture of two dice showing sixes on them (the combination known as "box cars"). Between these numbers and the "pass" and "don't pass" lines is a large area with the word "come" on it. Between this and the pass and don't pass lines is an area marked "field" with the numbers: 2, 3, 4, 9, 10, 11, and 12.

In the corner of this layout, closest to the player and away from the center of the table, is a small area divided in two and marked: "Big 6" and "Big 8." In the center of the table is a betting area marked: "hardway bets," for numbers 4, 6, 8, and 10. And just above this center layout is an area marked "any 7."

Below the center hardway layout is a combination of symbols for one-roll bets, and to each side of this center layout are rows of two "circles," one beside the other in staggered formation, each circle alternatively marked with a "C" or "E"—all of which I will discuss later in this chapter.

♦| HOW THE GAME IS PLAYED |♦

Craps looks like a very complicated game, and indeed it can be. But, as you will shortly find out, it can also be a game as simple as you want to make it. Nevertheless, in order to understand its simplicities as well as complexities, it is quite important that you pay close attention to what I am saying and how each segment of this chapter relates to, and affects, the other aspects of the game. In particular, I will advise you to keep looking at the table layout as I introduce and explain each item in the game of Craps. This will allow you to visualize the game and will serve to clarify the information and descriptions that follow.

The casino game of Craps is played with a set of two perfectly balanced dice, red in color, each die with six faces numbered 1 through 6 by means of white dots. The game is played by tossing both dice from one of the short ends of the table to the other, making sure that both dice hit the opposite side wall of the table; payoffs are made based on the number combination displayed when the dice come to rest. The inside walls of the table are covered with a kind of serrated egg-carton foam, designed to make the dice bounce around to assure randomness.

Each throw of the dice is called a "roll." Players take turns rolling the dice, clockwise around the table, and the player rolling at any given time is called the "shooter." When a new shooter is given the dice, his or her first roll is called the "come out" roll. This begins a new series of rolls by that shooter, and lasts for as long as that shooter continues to make winning rolls (winning and losing rolls will be discussed shortly).

A new game in Craps begins with the come out roll. A come out roll can be made only if, either, the table is empty and a new player, or players, just walk up, or, if the game is already in progress, when the previous shooter fails to make a winning roll—more correctly known as "not making the point," or "seven out." A new game then begins with a new shooter.

If the current shooter does make his point, the dice are returned to him and he then begins the new come out roll. This is a continuation of that shooter's roll, although, technically, the come out roll identifies a new game about to begin.

When the shooter fails to make his or her point, the dice are then offered to the next player for a new come out roll, and the game continues in the same manner. The new shooter will be the person directly next to the left of the previous shooter. This person could be you right away, or not, depending which position around the table the dice are in when you come into the game.

On the come out roll, the pass line bet wins if the shooter rolls a 7 or an 11. The bet loses automatically if the shooter rolls 2, 3, or 12. This is known as "rolling craps." If the shooter rolls either 4, 5, 6, 8, 9, or 10, winning your bet now depends on whether the shooter will roll this same number again *before rolling any* 7. Rolling any of these numbers on the come out roll is called "establishing the point." Any number so rolled is thereafter referred to as the "point." Establishing a point is an event that happens as the immediate result of the come out roll, unless that come out roll results in 7, 11, 2, 3, or 12, in which case more rolls must be made until a point is established (more on this a little further on).

I must now mention a device that looks like a hockey puck, called "the puck." It is white on one side and black on the other, and is used by the dealers to identify the point. Once the point is established by the shooter, the dealer will move the puck to that point number and turn it white side up. The puck stays on this point until the shooter either makes his point or sevens out. When this happens the puck is moved to the don't come bar 12 area, and turned black side up. The significance of this device is only in tracking the game. White side up over a point indicates the game is in progress and that this box number is the point. Black side up means a new come out roll is about to take place.

♦| HOW TO BET |♦

As with all table games, you begin by changing your cash money into gaming chips. In Craps you do it by throwing your money on the table and yelling "change." If the table is playing well there will be a lot of people crowding around and a lot of noise, so make sure you yell out. Also, it is a good idea to wait and ask for change between rolls of the dice.

In Craps, winning or losing depends on a variety of different possible outcomes on any roll of the two dice, and on which of these possibilities you bet. The two dice can produce many different number combinations; some can be made several ways, others only one way. For example, the number 6 can be rolled by two dice as follows: 5/1, 4/2, 3/3, 2/4, and 1/5. But the number 2 can only be rolled one way: 1/1. Numbers such as 6, which can be rolled several ways, don't pay as much as numbers that can be rolled only one way, unless you are betting that the number will be rolled in a specific way, such as 3/3 (more on this in the section on Hard Ways). All winning payoffs are, therefore, determined by the frequency in which any two-dice number combinations can be rolled. Generally, the harder the combination is to roll, the more it will pay, and vice versa.

Although really taking advantage of the many betting options can involve a considerable degree of mastery, in its simplest form Craps is a game where players bet either that the shooter *will* make winning rolls, or that he or she *will not* make winning rolls.

Betting that the shooter will make winning rolls is called betting "with the shooter" (also called "betting right"), and betting that the shooter will not make winning rolls is called "betting against the shooter" (also called "betting wrong").

To bet with the shooter, you place your bet in an area marked "pass line," known as making a "line bet." The so-called pass line is a strip on the table layout marked by two lines roughly two inches wide that rim the entire table layout across from the Boxman. To bet against the shooter, you place your bet in an area marked "don't pass." This area is also a strip on the table layout, and it rims the table directly above the pass line.

No matter what stage the game is in, whether on the come out roll, or in progress, you can jump in immediately and place any bets. The only exception is the bet called the "pass line bet with odds," which can be made only on the come out roll. You can, however, bet with the shooter even while the game is in progress, by placing a pass line bet *without odds*. This is done by placing your gaming chips halfway over one of the two lines framing the pass line area.

Before the new shooter rolls the dice on his or her come out roll, there are a variety of bets that can be made. The easiest and most common bets to make are the above-mentioned pass line and don't pass line bet. But after a point is established by the shooter, you can then place an additional bet behind your pass line bet. This is called "taking odds."

In most casinos you can bet up to double the amount of your pass line bet. This is called "taking full odds." Some casinos offer up to 10-times odds, and this simply means that you can bet up to 10 times the amount of your pass line bet once a point is established.

Betting the don't pass line is the exact opposite of betting the pass line. If you do this on the come out roll, your don't pass bet wins if the shooter rolls any Craps—2 or 3 (ties on 12)—and loses automatically on any 7 and 11. Tying on 12 simply means that there is no decision—your don't pass bet neither wins nor loses, merely stays in limbo till a decision is reached on subsequent rolls.

If the shooter establishes a point, your don't pass bet stays in action, but for you to win your bet the shooter must roll a 7 before making his point. Therefore, a don't pass bet wins if the shooter fails to make his point but loses if the shooter does make the point. You can also take odds on a don't pass bet.

A don't pass bet is not a bad bet, but I do not recommend it for the casual player since it requires a solid grasp of odds mathematics as well as considerable game acumen. Betting with the shooter is a far easier method to grasp in a short time, and offers many more advantages. For the remainder of this chapter, therefore, I will confine all play and bet suggestions to the right way bets.

Once the shooter establishes a point, a whole range of betting options opens up in addition to all the bets available on the come out roll. However, before I continue, it is important that we understand the concept of "true odds." The fact is that casinos do not pay off winning bets at true odds but rather at reduced odds. This is what provides the House with its healthy edge over the player, a situation most acutely visible in the one roll bets.

A payoff at true odds on a bet is a payoff that precisely matches the likelihood of a particular two-dice number combination being rolled. For example, since the two-dice number combination of either 2 or 12 will be rolled, on average, once in every 36 rolls, payoff at true odds for bets on these rolls would be 36:1. You will notice, however, that casinos only pay off on such bets at 30:1.

These variances provide the House with an overall 16.6 percent edge over the player on such bets. Bets on 11 and 3 also provide this same House edge. To better understand this, think of how many possible ways there are for rolling any of the numbers available in the game of Craps. No, I don't expect you to be mathematical whiz kids, so here's the count:

The number 2 can be rolled only one way—1/1; same number for 12—6/6; numbers 3 and 11 can each be rolled in two ways; numbers 4 and 10 can each be rolled in three ways; numbers 5 and 9 can each be rolled in four ways; numbers 6 and 8 can each be rolled in five ways and the number 7 can be rolled in six ways.

It is easy to see, for instance, how the number 7 can be either your friend or your foe in Craps. The number 7 is rolled, on the average, once in each 6 rolls. Therefore, on the come out roll, betting the pass line bet is a good bet indeed, since if a 7 is rolled this bet wins. It is an even better bet because it also wins if an 11 is rolled. Since there are six ways to roll a 7, and two ways to roll an 11, there are eight chances out of 36 that a 7 or 11 will be rolled—about once in every 4.5 rolls.

But once a point is established, the odds turn against the players, since a 7 can be rolled in more ways and more frequently than any of the other numbers, including the established point. And if the 7 is rolled, all right way bets lose. This disadvantage for the player is offset by players who are smart enough to take odds on their pass line bets and come bets. Taking advantage of the full odds reduces the House edge over the player to about 0.85 percent on such bets, as opposed to about 1.4 percent on such bets without odds.

Now that we are clear on what true odds are and why casinos do not pay them on all bets, I will explore in greater detail some of the bets that can be made once the point has been established, including bets that do pay off at true odds and why.

◆ | COME BETS | ◆

A popular, as well as advantageous, bet is the "come" bet. To make it, you place your gaming chips inside the large area marked "come" on the table layout. This bet can be made only after the shooter has established a point and must be made between rolls of the dice.

The come bet works in much the same way as the pass line bet. On the first roll after you have placed your chips in the come bet area, your bet will win even money if a 7 or 11 is rolled and lose if any Craps is rolled. However, you must remember that if a 7 is rolled, all pass line bets automatically lose. Therefore, assuming you have made a pass line bet, you are *not* making the come bet because you want the shooter to roll a 7, but because you think he or she will roll other numbers for some time.

If an 11—not a 7—is rolled on this first roll after you have made your come bet, the come bet wins even money and there is no action on any of the other bets, except for those players who bet the 11 as a one roll bet, or any one roll bets that include an 11. If you made a come bet and an 11 is rolled immediately, you can either pick up your winnings and place your original come bet again, or, by letting the chips stay in the come bet area, bet both your original bet plus your winnings on the next roll. This is called "let it ride," and you should call these words out to the dealer to let him know that this is what you want to do. This same result can be achieved if you reach into the come bet area and stack all your chips. This is a quick indication to the dealer that you are letting it ride.

If neither 7, 11, 2, 3, or 12 is rolled after you have made a come bet, this can *only* mean that one of the box numbers has been rolled instead. That is the desired objective of making a come bet. When it happens, the dealer will move your bet to whatever box number has been rolled. From now on, winning this bet depends on the shooter rolling that same box number again before rolling a 7. This box number then becomes your "come number."

Once your original come bet has been moved to the rolled come number, you cannot take it down—again the same rules that apply to the initial pass line or don't pass line bets—and it will stay there until either that come number is rolled before a 7, in which case it wins, or a 7 is rolled first, in which case it will lose.

After your original come bet has been moved to a rolled come number, and at any time during the game before that come number is rolled again or a 7 is rolled, you can take odds. This is called "odds on the come," and you do it by throwing the amount of your odds bet onto the table in front of you and calling out "odds on the come" to the dealer. Taking odds on your come number works exactly the same as taking odds on your pass line bet. If the casino you are in offers double odds—most common in all major casinos—you can bet up to double the amount of your come bet as your odds bet.

Here's a short table showing come bet payoffs on double odds:

Come Number	Payoff	Cash Example
4 or 10	2:1	$10 wins $20
5 or 9	3:2	$10 wins $15
6 or 8	6:5	$10 wins $12

If your come bet wins with odds, as shown above, you will also be paid even money on the original come bet.

Therefore, if your original come bet is $5, the come number turns out to be the number 4, you take double odds of $10, and the number 4 is rolled again before a 7 is rolled, you will be paid $20 for your odds bet plus $5 for your original come bet for a total net winnings of $25 ($40 gross, when counting the amount of your total bet—$5 on the come plus $10 double odds, which you also get to keep).

You can make a come bet as many times as you like throughout the course of the current game. Each time you make a come bet, the same rules apply. Of course, if you continue to make come bets, it is possible that pretty soon you will have come bets on all the box numbers. At this point making further come bets is counterproductive.

Should this happen, wait for one of your come bets to win, and then you can either let it ride—in other words "press" your bet, done by calling out, "Press it," to the dealer—or take your winnings and make another come bet.

Very often when you have many come bets and make yet another one, the box number rolled will be one on which you already have a come bet. This is called "off and on," meaning that the come bet you already have on that number wins and comes off—you collect your winnings— and the come bet you just made goes on to that same number. Come bet winnings are placed by the dealer in the come bet area closest to where you are standing. You *must* pick up your winnings immediately, because if the dice are rolled before you collect your chip, those chips will automatically be considered as your next come bet.

As often happens, if the point is rolled immediately after you have made the come bet in the come bet area, the pass line bets win and a new game begins. But your come bet now goes on to what was the previous point number, which now becomes your come number for the next series of rolls. However, this come bet will now lose if a 7 is rolled on the new come out roll. This also applies if you still have other come bets left.

If you still have such other come bets already on the board and have already taken odds on them, only the original come bet will lose if a 7 is rolled on the new come out roll. The odds are returned to you. You can also achieve the same result by callng out,"Down on the odds." This means you are telling the dealer that you no longer want these come bet odds to play, and he will return all your odds money to you.

You can also call your come bet odds "off" by calling out, "Odds off," which means the odds will not be in action but the bet will stay on the board along with your initial come bet. You should, however, remember that come bet odds are automatically off on the come out roll, when such a come out roll takes place immediately after that same shooter has just made the point. This is the only time that come bets and odds remain on the board for a new come out roll. If that shooter did *not* make the point, these come bets and odds would have lost.

Odds or bets that have been called off are identified by the dealer with a small marker chip with the words "off" printed on it; this marker chip is placed by the dealer over whatever bet, or odds on a bet, have been called off by that player. Bets that are called off are not at risk and will not win or lose regardless of what numbers are rolled while they are off.

To reactivate any bet or odds that have been called off, all you need to do is call out, "Working," and whatever bet has been so identified is now back in action again.

Taking your come bet odds down, or calling them off, can be done any time during the game but is quite inappropriate on a new come out roll after the shooter has just made the point. As I stated earlier, in this case your come bet odds are not at risk—unless you chose to put them at risk—so there's no reason to call them off or down. You can, however, put your come bet *odds*—as well as your original come bet—at risk on the come out roll by calling out, "Odds on." This means that you have chosen to put not just your original come bet at risk on the come out roll—automatically so—but have also decided to put the come bet odds at risk. These odds are then called "free odds," and if your come number is rolled on the come out roll to become the new point number, your bet will pay off at true odds. However, both your original come bet and the free odds will now lose if a 7 is rolled on the come out roll. It is therefore not a good idea to do this.

If another box number is rolled—one on which you do not have a come bet, with or without free odds—that box number now becomes the new point, and your come bets remain in play to win or lose under the same rules as when you originally made the bets.

Calling any of your come bets, including odds, down or off can be done at any time during the game before either a winning or losing result is achieved. The same can be done for all bets and odds, except the original pass line and don't pass bets. Taking your bets down also applies to any pass line or don't pass odds, which you can pick up yourself at any time during the game and put back again as you wish prior to the point being made or a 7 being rolled.

◆| DON'T COME BETS |◆

As with the pass line and don't pass line bets, "don't come" bets are the exact opposite of come bets. To make this bet you place your chips in the area marked "don't come bar 12." If the shooter now rolls a 7 or 11, the bet loses automatically. Your bet wins if the shooter rolls any craps, and ties if the shooter rolls a 12. As explained earlier, such a tie is simply a no-result and the bet stays for further rolls until a result is achieved. Barring a payoff on 12 on don't come and don't pass bets is what provides the house with its edge on these bets.

If the shooter rolls any box number—now referred to as the "don't come number"—your don't come bet is moved into a small area behind this number. Winning now depends on whether the shooter will roll a 7 before rolling that same number again.

Odds bets are made the same way as on the come numbers, but, again, they work in exactly the opposite fashion as the come bets. In simple terms, you have to bet more to win less. It is not a good idea to make don't come bets if you are making pass line bets. Doing this is betting against yourself. For practical purposes, I will not recommend don't come bets for the same reasons I have previously advised against the don't pass bets, and will therefore avoid further mention of them as meaningful strategy suggestions.

◆ | HARD WAYS | ◆

Another bet available to you while the game is in progress is a "hard ways" bet. This is a bet that the shooter will roll a 4, 6, 8, or 10 as a pair of doubles—2 + 2, 3 + 3, 4 + 4, or 5 + 5, respectively—before rolling it any other way. This is known as rolling the numbers the "hard way." The singular term "hard way" applies to any number so rolled; the plural "hardways" applies to bets on more than one such number, or as a term to describe all such hard way options. To make this bet, you throw the amount of your bet into the center of the table and call out to the Stickman where you want the hard way bet to go.

For example, if you wish to bet the hard 4 for $10, you will throw two $5 chips in the center of the table and call out, "Ten on hard four." The Stickman will then move your bet to the center of the table into the area marked "hard ways," and place it over the number 4. To win this bet, and any other hardways bet, the shooter must roll this number in a paired combination before rolling it any other way.

There is only one way that any hard way number can be rolled the hard way. Any other combination rolled for these numbers is called "rolled easy." You can bet just one, two, three, or all the four hardways numbers, but to win the shooter must roll that hard way number the hard way. If rolled easy, the bets lose.

Hard 4 and hard 10 pay 8:1, while hard 6 and hard 8 pay 10:1. It is, of course, less common to roll double combinations of these numbers than it is to roll them in other combinations. For example, out of 36 possible number combinations, there are four out of five ways each to roll 6 and 8 easy, but only one hard way. That's why 6 and 8 pay so well for the hard ways bet. And 4 and 10 can be rolled easy only two ways each, but hard only one way each. Since hard way bets on 4 and 10 are fractionally better than bets on 6 and 8, they pay less. But the difference is so small, and these bets so unattractive from an overall strategy point, that it makes little difference in the reality of play.

All hardways bets lose automatically when the shooter sevens out. However, if the shooter does make the point, all hardways bets will ride on the new come out roll unless you call them off or down. On the new come out roll any one hard way bet will lose if that number is rolled easy, but all hardways bets will lose if a 7 is rolled. It is typically a good idea to call your hard ways bets off—by yelling, "Hard ways off"—on the come out roll, and then, when you wish to place them in action again, to call out, "Hard ways working," at that time. Often the dealers will automatically do it for you once they know that you play this way consistently. As with all bets, other than the original pass line and don't pass bets, hard way bets can be called off or down any time during the game.

♦| "BUY," "LAY," AND "PLACE" BETS |♦

In addition to playing any box number as the established point, or as your come number, you also can make other direct bets on any one, or more, of the box numbers. With the possible exception of the place bets, these are not good bets overall and I will therefore only identify them without going into great detail.

♦| BUY BETS |♦

To make a "buy" bet, as well as any "lay" or "place" bets, you throw out the amount of your bet onto the table in front of you and call out to the dealer the number on which you want the bet to go—for example, "Buy the 4." Such bets are identified by a small marker chip with the word "buy" printed on it, which is placed by the dealer over the bet. Buy bets are often called "do come buy bets," and are always *off* on the come out roll. The house advantage over the player on buy bets is roughly 4.8 percent. This bet will win if the bought number is rolled before a 7, and lose otherwise.

Payoffs are the same as for odds bets on the pass line or come, but the house will charge you a 5 percent commission for this kind of bet payable at the time you make your bet. The house charges the commission because such bets are paid at the same rate as come bet and pass line odds, and the amount of this commission is the payment you make to the house for buying the odds payoff.

Buy bets remain in play until the number is rolled, or until the shooter sevens out. As with other bets, buy bets can be called off and on or down at any time during the game until the number you have bought is rolled, in which case the buy bet wins, or the shooter sevens out first, in which case the buy bet will lose.

It is best to buy numbers in multiples of $25, which minimizes the commission cost. On a $25 buy bet the 5 percent commission is $1.25, but because casinos do not pay in fractions they do not take bets in fractions either; therefore, your commission will only be $1, the same as for a $20 buy bet. So you not only save the quarter, but you increase your winnings by $5 over the normally recommended $20 buy bet. This works the same for all multiples of $25. Of course, the reverse is also true; if you make a buy bet for less than $20, you will still have to pay the $1 commission—more, in fact, than you should pay on bets below $20.

◆| LAY BETS |◆

"Lay" bets are practically the exact opposite of buy bets. They are often called "don't come buy bets" because any lay-bet number will lose if rolled before a 7, but win if a 7 is rolled first—the opposite to buy bets. If you make this bet, you are betting with the odds against you. For example, if you lay either the 4 or the 10, you must bet $40 to win $20. The house edge on these bets is around 3.2 percent, and the small benefit to players lies in the fact that the 5 percent commission is charged by the house on the winnings, and not on the amount of the initial bet, as in buy bets. A lay bet is *always on*.

◆| PLACE BETS |◆

Place bets can be made on any box number at any time during the game in progress, and are paid at true odds. This means that a place bet on 4 or 10 will pay off at 9:5 odds instead of the 8:4 normally paid. Numbers 5 and 9 will pay at 7:5 instead of the normal 6:4, and numbers 6 or 8 will pay off at odds 7:6 instead of the usual 6:5. Outside of the come, and in some instances the don't come bets, a place bet on 6 or 8 is one of the best bets available in Craps, because it reduces the House advantage to a mere 1.5 percent, roughly the same as for the pass line bets.

The overall House edge on all place bets combined is about 4 percent, and players who make these bets are best advised to make them in multiples of five chips, six for 6 and 8, based around the table minimum bet requirement. (A chip is generally considered to have a value of $1, so five chips is $5 and six chips $6, unless you are betting higher limits; in that case the same principle will apply—five $5 chips will equal a bet of $25, six $5 chips a bet of $30, and so on.)

A place bet is *off* on the come out roll, unless the player requests otherwise. If you call this bet "on," the dealer will place a small marker chip with the words "on" written on it over your bet. Any place bet will win if rolled before a 7 and lose otherwise. The bet stays on the table until either a win or loss decision is achieved and cannot be taken down although it can be called off and on.

◆| "ALL ACROSS" |◆

A popular bet is one where you cover all the available box numbers with one bet—this is a bet called "all across." You make this bet by throwing the amount of the total bet on the table in front of you and calling out, "All across," to the dealer. This is a good bet, because you can cover all the box numbers at once, in addition to whatever point has been established. All such bets play the same way as if they had been come bets, but pay off as place bets. You can also begin to win immediately when any of the box numbers is rolled and you don't have to wait for the number to be rolled twice, as in come bets.

On a $5 minimum table, the minimum bet for all across is $27, unless the point is 6 or 8, in which case it is $26—$5 each on 4, 5, 9, and 10, and $6 each on the 6 and 8, less the appropriate amount for whatever box number is the point.

You can also make this bet in multiples of the amounts indicated above. By making your bets all across you are betting, in effect, that the shooter will roll for quite a while, hitting many numbers other than 7. These bets continue to win for as long as the numbers the bets cover are rolled, and lose when a 7 is rolled. You can call these bets off and on, but must call *all* the all across numbers off and on at the same time, not individually.

This bet can get expensive, especially if the shooter sevens out soon after you make the bet and before rolling at least some of your numbers once. For this reason, management of this bet is very important. The skill involved here is in pressing your bets, and calling them off when, in your judgment, the shooter is about to seven out, and then on again if you think the shooter is about to roll numbers once more.

The word "crap shoot" really applies here, because these off and on judgments are quite difficult to pinpoint from an overall strategy advice position, and their success or failure will depend on how each individual player reacts to the situations at that particular table at that particular time. But pressing the bet is an easy bit of advice, because it is only by doing it that you can make a lot of money fast in Craps, especially on an all across bet.

"Pressing" a bet is a fundamental concept in gambling, and simply means that you are increasing the amount of your original bet, when it wins, by the amount of your win, or a fraction thereof. This concept is so important in Craps that playing Craps without pressing at least some of your bets at some time will be an exercise in losing money.

Pressing your bets is important because you can double your win expectation while at the same time risking only your original bet. This is the best way to make some money in Craps. If you press and hit, take the win; then, if you hit again, press again, and so on. When you lose, go back to your original bet. You can press any bet during the course of the game, except the pass line and don't pass bets, or any odds, unless these odds are part of a winning come bet, in which case you can press the entire come bet, including winning odds, by calling, "Press it." Pressing bets can be done in any gambling table game.

♦ | "BIG 6" AND "BIG 8" | ♦

"Big 6" means a 6 in any combination. "Big 8" means an 8 in any combination. Both bets pay even money. These are not one roll bets, but work exactly the same as place bets on 6 and 8, except that bets on Big 6 and Big 8 pay much less.

If you ever see anyone making bets on Big 6 or Big 8, consider such a player casino fodder. It's silly players like those that casinos love to see at the Craps table, because they know this is a prize sucker. Big 6 and Big 8 bets can be made after the point is established, and pay off if a 6 or 8—depending on which number the bet is on—is rolled before any 7. Bets can be placed on either or both numbers. The house edge on these bets is over 9 percent.

But 6 and 8 are box numbers, and can be bet either as a come bet, or a place bet. Place bets on 6 and 8 win and lose in the same way as Big 6 and Big 8, but wins on 6 and 8 as place bets are paid at 7:6. This reduces the house edge to about 1.5 percent, roughly 6 times lower than the same bet on Big 6 or Big 8! So why in the world would anyone ever bet the Big 6 or Big 8? Still, many people do. They are silly players, not smart players.

◆| ONE ROLL BETS |◆

One roll bets are exactly that—bets for which winning and losing outcomes are decided on one particular roll of the dice. There are several such bets available in Craps, and they are universally bad. Not only are such bets difficult to win on, but even when they do win you will be paid off at reduced odds and not the true odds.

On these bets you are not only giving up a sizable edge to the house in making the bet in the first place, but are also giving up a large chunk of your winnings by receiving less than the odds to which you should be entitled.

One roll bets can be divided into two groups: "field" bets and "proposition" bets.

◆| FIELD BETS |◆

Of all the one roll bets, field bets are probably the best of a bad lot. To make a field bet you simply put your money in the area on the table layout marked "field." When you make a field bet you are betting that on the next roll the shooter will roll any one of the so-called "field numbers"— 2, 3, 4, 9, 10, 11, or 12. If the shooter rolls any of these numbers, you win. Number 2 and number 12 pay 2:1; all other field bets pay even money. (In some casinos 12 will pay 3:1, in others 2 will pay 3:1—though both are quite uncommon in modern casino play.) If the shooter rolls any other number, these bets lose. Again, these are one roll bets only, and each subsequent roll of the dice is a new game for these field bets, as with all other one roll bets. If you wish to keep your field bet working, you must put up a new bet for each roll.

◆| PROPOSITION BETS |◆

These are among the worst bets in Craps, but many players bet them because of what appear to be, on the surface, terrific payoffs. I'm not advising you never to bet them, but I am advising you to be aware not only of how difficult they are to win on, but that in betting them you are giving up a substantial edge to the House. On these bets you can make one-roll wagers on: "snake eyes," "box cars," "ace-deuce," "yo-eleven," "any seven," "any craps," and "horn." These are all popular slang terms for particular combinations of the dice, and you can bet any or all of them.

Snake eyes	a pair of ones, also known as a pair of aces: 1 + 1. It pays 15:1.
Box cars	a pair of sixes: 6 + 6. It pays 30:1.
Ace-deuce	an ace (1) and a two. It pays 15:1.
Yo-eleven	an 11. It pays 15:1.
Any seven	a 7, in any combination. It pays 5:1. Although it is very rare, in some casinos you can still make a side bet on 7 by calling for a specific 7 combination, say: 5 + 2. This is called "on the hop." In fact, such a bet can be made on any of twenty-one possible combinations of the available numbers and generally pays 14:1, depending on the rules of the casino which offers such side bets. (Don't look for these bets; they are a waste of your money and time.)
Any craps	a bet on "snake eyes," "box cars," and "ace-deuce."
Horn	any craps (2, 3, 12) and 11.

The best advice I can give you is to avoid any of these
one roll bets. The pass line bet with full odds and the come
bet with full odds are much smarter bets, so much so that
wagering your money on the difficult-to-hit propositions is
just a silly waste. Once you have experienced the game of
Craps and gained a more thorough understanding of how
the game works, not merely in theory but in practice, you
can become more adventurous and begin to make certain
judgments during the flow of the game. Generally, however,
one-roll bets are called "sucker bets," and that, I think, says
it all.

◆ | "C" AND "E" | ◆

Often you will hear Craps players call for "C and E,"
meaning they want to bet both the "any craps and 11." Most
of the time this bet is made on the come out roll, but many
players will also take either any craps alone or the joint C
and E bet during the game, especially when they have a
large bet on the come. This is done because a bet in the
come area, before it makes it to a rolled number, will lose if
any craps is rolled. Consequently, betting either any craps
alone or C and E jointly on the come out roll or during the
game is a sort of insurance bet. You're not betting specifically that craps or 11 will be rolled, but to protect your pass
line bet on the come out roll in the event that any craps—
2, 3, or 12— is rolled, or for the same reason to protect your
come bet during the game.

On the come out roll a bet on "C"—any craps—will win
if any craps is rolled and lose otherwise; this bet will pay
off at 8:1. A bet on "E" will win only if an 11 is rolled, and
lose otherwise; it pays off at 15:1. A bet on C and E jointly
will win if any craps or 11 is rolled on the come out roll; if
it wins, it will stay in action for the next roll until another
decision is reached or you call the bet down, and will lose

if a 7 is rolled on the come out roll. A bet on C and E jointly will pay off at whatever odds apply to whichever of the two events was rolled.

If you bet C and E jointly during the game, after a point has been established, you should do so only if you have also just made a new come bet. Since the new come bet will lose if any craps is rolled, this C and E bet is good insurance. You should, however, make the C and E bet in proportion to the amount of your bet at risk. Your C and E joint bet will also win if an 11 is rolled, as well as any craps, but if any craps is rolled on the come out roll your pass line bet will lose; and if any craps is rolled on the next roll after you have just made a new come bet, that bet will also lose, so only the 11 can realistically provide you with a bonus pay when making this kind of bet. It is therefore a long-shot bet and should be treated not as a good one roll bet, but only as an added bet for the purpose of insuring one or more of your other, more favorable, bets, and only in the two circumstances I have just described.

♦| SIMPLE STRATEGY |♦

My brief outline of the game of Craps is merely a simple introduction to what can be a very complex game. If you are eager to get deeper into the mechanics of the game, there are plenty of books that deal exclusively with Craps and offer exhaustive and detailed betting strategies.

Indeed, some offer so much information that the point of the game can get lost within the pages and can easily make the game seem more confusing that it really is. To keep my advice in the spirit of simplicity and at the same time give you a sufficient mastery of Craps for any casual gaming, here is some quick basic advice:

1. Always bet the pass line. Start with the table minimum and, if you are winning, press your bet by half

the amount of your win each time you have a winner. Look for tables whose minimum bet requirements allow you to reach a progression in multiples of three chips without requiring you to spend more than 25 percent of your initial starting session bankroll on any one bet. Each time you hit a loser, bet half your previous bet, including half of your previous odds bet; if it loses again, bet half that on the next roll until you reach the table minimum. Stay at the table minimum until you start winning again, and then press your bets as before. Avoid the don't pass bet. It will complicate your game and will offer you less enjoyment and profit.

2. Always take full odds on the pass line and come bets. Most casinos offer double odds, so take them. If you are in a casino that offers triple odds, or 10-times odds, start with double odds, and increase your odds if you're winning by doubling your previous odds bet for each win, until you reach the table's odds maximum. Likewise, in these triple and 10-times odds casinos, decrease your odds bet by the same amount of your previous increase after each loss.

3. On the come out roll always bet "C and E" (any craps and eleven). This will protect your pass line bet if the shooter rolls any craps, and give you a winning bonus if the shooter rolls an 11. For example, if you're betting, say, $5 on the pass line, bet $1 each on C and E.

4. Make two come bets in addition to your pass line bet. This way you will have three amounts in action: your pass line bet and odds (with its corresponding point), and your two come bets and odds. This is a good way to start your play, and it won't hurt you a great deal if you hit a cold table and lose a few turns.

5. Since Craps is a notoriously streaky game, recognizing hot and cold streaks is of paramount importance. If your table, and the shooter, are hot, bet into this streak by increasing the amounts of your bets and odds, perhaps by double the progressions I suggested earlier. Hot streaks occur frequently, but may only last a few rolls, so you must constantly pay attention to what is happening during the course of a Craps game. Such hot streaks defy all laws of probability and, therefore, normal betting situations need to be modified to maximize your win potential. Conversely, cold streaks also occur, often lasting seemingly longer than hot streaks. When this happens, it is also important that you *do not* bet into them, but reduce your bets to the table minimum until such time as you spot a hot streak again.

6. If you're feeling good about the shooters on this table, place the 6 and 8 in multiples of $6 each. This will provide you the best payoff when either number is rolled. You can do this in addition to any come bet, so long as neither of your come bets is, at this time, on the 6 or 8. When the bet wins, press it; when it wins again call for "same bet"—which tells the dealer that you want your winnings but want to retain the current amount of your bet in action. If that shooter continues to do well, bet the all across and cover all the numbers. In this case don't bet the come; if you already have come bets in action, simply place the box numbers you still have not covered. Then just wait and wish for the shooter to roll anything except a 7. When you win on any of the numbers you have bets on, press your bet on that number. If it hits again, take the winnings and let the rest ride. And so on for all your numbers.

7. Don't bet field, Big 6, Big 8, hardways, or any one roll bets. These bets can easily eat you up and dis-

tract you from making your other bets properly. The only exception may be an occasional hard way bet, in the event that you have already made good profit and can therefore bet with House money and have spotted a trend toward paired combinations. But don't bet more than the table minimum at any one time, and if your hard way bet loses, quickly stop making them or you can get caught in the hardways bet trap.

8. Manage your money. The racks on Craps tables—the rail—offer an easy way to keep track of your stake and your winnings. Keep an eye out on how much you have. If you are winning, bet more, because by that time you are betting with the casino's money.

It is not unusual to see a lot of money bet on any single roll of the dice, especially if the table is full of players and the dice are hot. It is quite common for tables to win or lose several million dollars in a few hours. I have witnessed people who come in on a hot roll, put $5,000 or $10,000 in cash on the pass line, and in a few minutes walk away with several hundred thousand dollars. And I have also seen such bettors lose.

However, it is a common mistake to think that Craps is only for the high rollers. Many casinos offer small-limit games, starting with a $1 minimum, and some casinos even offer 25-cent craps. Of course how much you win depends on how much you bet. It's all relative. If you bet $1 with $2 odds, you won't win as much as if you were betting $5 with $10 odds, but then again, you don't lose as much either. Ultimately the amounts you can reasonably wager comes down to the size of your bankroll for that session.

Even if you visit a casino only once and want to try craps, by following the simple suggestions I have offered in this chapter, you will have a much better chance of winning money than otherwise and you will certainly enjoy the game more. Craps is a fascinating game and can quickly capture your continued interest. And even if you are already a regular casino visitor and may even have played Craps before, keeping these suggestions in mind will make you a smarter player.

6
ROULETTE

Of all the games offered in the modern casino, Roulette and Baccarat are perhaps the games that most evoke the mystique of the sophisticated Continental gambler. When you see James Bond gambling in the movies, he is almost always seen in the high-toned casinos of Monte Carlo or the private clubs in London or Paris, and invariably the game you see him playing is either Roulette or Baccarat. The way these two games are portrayed in such motion pictures gives one the impression that they are meant only for the sophisticated, titled, blue-blooded, wealthy European high roller. Far from it.

Perhaps the reason we associate Roulette and Baccarat with this European gaming scene is because both games are European in origin. They have been around for centuries in practically unaltered form and did not make their way to the Americas until quite late in their history. Since, in earlier times, only the upper-class rich could afford to play them, a glamorized image of these games of chance seems to have outlasted all the kings, counts, dukes, and others whose exuberant and spendthrift lifestyles invested them with their aura of sophistication. Today only the game of Baccarat comes close to living up to its elitist image. Roulette long ago came to be a game that wasn't left merely to an upper-crust crowd.

Perhaps because of its sheer simplicity, Roulette found a place in the early American West. Old West ghost towns provide proof of this game's popularity among our pioneering ancestors. In some of those old ghost towns you can walk into the saloon and still see the rusting Roulette wheel sitting where it was abandoned, the layout covered in dust and old gaming chips lying around.

♦| **HOW TO RECOGNIZE ROULETTE** |♦

The game of Roulette is easily spotted in the modern casino because it is the only active table game which uses a mechanical element as a key ingredient. The majority of all the other table games offered in the modern casino are card-based (Craps being the exception), and therefore require merely a dealer and players.

Roulette employs a large wheel, not unlike a wagon wheel, mounted within the table itself. The craftsmanship of a Roulette wheel is truly marvelous. It is made of wood with a central metal core, usually of brass, and is sunken in a "dish" that looks like the bottom half of an open barrel. It is perfectly balanced and needs only the slightest touch to start it spinning. Around the outer edge of this wheel are pockets numbered 1 through 36, arranged nonsequentially, in alternating colors of black and red.

In addition, the American Roulette wheel has two more pockets—one "0" (zero) and one "00" (double zero). These are the "House numbers," and the House wins all bets if the ball happens to land on either (I will explain the exceptions a little further on). These two House numbers are green in color, and they provide the House edge. The European versions of Roulette only use the extra 0 (single zero), and this one fact substantially alters the House edge and considerably favors the player, compared to the American version. Some casinos do offer European Roulette, but mostly with high betting requirements.

The wheel itself is a delicate instrument. The accuracy of the Roulette game is entirely dependent on the perfect balance of the wheel. Even the tiniest imbalance will result in what is known as a "biased wheel," which can favor either the House or the smart and observant player. In some instances unscrupulous operators have been known to weight the wheel in order to win consistently, often from some targeted player. This is, of course, cheating, which is now all but impossible in the modern casino. The way the game is set up, its win percentage is so much in favor of the House anyway that casino owners do not have to cheat to win. And no modern casino operator would ever risk his gaming license just to win a few dollars from Roulette or any other gambling game.

The balance of the Roulette wheel is precarious, and for this reason it is often protected by enclosure in strong plastic casings, with even stronger side protectors. The unwary player, if seen leaning up against it, will be quickly advised not to do so.

In addition to the Roulette wheel itself, the Roulette table features the game's layout. As in Craps and Blackjack, this layout is painted on the felt that covers the table and indicates the betting possibilities. This is where players lay their bets. Larger Roulette tables have two such layouts, with the wheel mounted square in the middle. Players sit in comfortable chairs all around this table layout, except where the *croupier*—French word for the dealer—stands, which is the side of the Roulette table that faces the Rou-

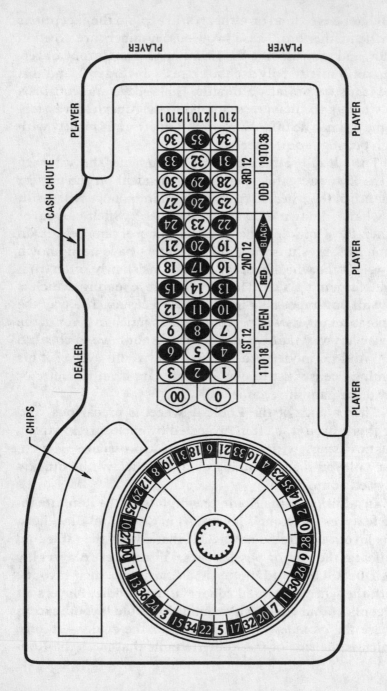

The complete layout for American Roulette as it appears in the casino.

lette pit. The croupier is a casino employee, in uniform, who spins the ball, pays off winners, and collects losing bets—a dealer just like all the others in the casino.

The layout is rectangular in shape. In the center is a red and black grid bearing the numbers 1 through 36, which correspond to the numbers of the Roulette wheel and appear on the layout in 12 rows of three, numbered sequentially.

The left side of the layout also displays the two House numbers 0 and 00, in green. This makes a total of 38 available numbers, any of which can be bet on, either singly or in groups.

Additionally, the layout displays areas along one side marked: 1 through 18, and 19 through 36, which refer to those groups of numbers; first 12, second 12 and third 12 (i.e., 1 through 12, 2 through 24, and 25 through 36, known as "squares"); odd and even, which refer to all odd or all even numbers on the wheel; and black and red, which refer to all numbers bearing that color. The final area available for bets is the first row of 12, second row of 12 and the third row of 12, known as "columns," which, unlike the squares, are nonsequential.

♦| HOW TO BET |♦

Roulette is an extremely simple game. The wheel, with numbered pockets mounted inside the sunken dish, is spun. Then the croupier places a small white ball into a groove around the rim of the dish and spins it in the opposite direction to the spin of the wheel. Gravity eventually causes the ball to fall onto the spinning wheel, where it bounces around until it comes to rest in one of the numbered pockets. Winning and losing depend on where the ball lands and which bets players have made prior to the spin. Each spin of the wheel is a new game.

All bets are paid before the next spin, and all new bets must be made before the next spin. However, players can often continue to make bets right up to just before the white ball drops down and starts bouncing around the spinning wheel, which the croupier will indicate by calling out, "No more bets." Roulette is also the only casino game, apart from reel slots, where players are mere spectators and can make no decisions to affect the outcome of the game.

When you approach a Roulette table, the first thing you do is change your money into Roulette gaming chips. Unlike gaming chips used in all other table games, Roulette gaming chips show no denominational value. In all the other table games, if you buy a $5 chip you will get a red chip with "$5" printed on it. When you buy Roulette chips, the value of each chip is determined either by the value you specify each such chip to have, or automatically by the value corresponding to that table's minimum betting requirement. For example, say the table minimum is fifty-cent chips. This means that if you change $20 and do not specify the value of the Roulette chips, the croupier will automatically give you forty gaming chips, each of which has a value of fifty cents. However, you can specify the value of these chips.

If instead of fifty-cent value you want each chip to have a value of $1, all you have to do is ask the dealer for twenty dollars in $1 chips. By doing this you are increasing the value of the roulette chips from the table's minimum. You can specify that the chips you buy have any value from the table minimum up to $5 each. If you specify $5 value chips, then you will get the red chips with the $5 value printed on them. These are the same chips you will normally get in all the other table games. If you intend to bet $25 chips, or $100 chips, the same applies.

The reason for this system is because most Roulette players will only bet $1 chips or chips of lesser values. Of course, this does not prevent you from stacking the chips up. Even if you bought $20 in fifty-cent chips and decided to bet them all on the one number, it would be perfectly okay to do so. In that case you would just stack them all up one on top of the other on the number you wanted to bet. If you do this the dealer may suggest that you simply bet four red $5 chips instead, but it makes no difference to the game. In fact, no one will bother you or question any of your decisions. All the casino requires is that you make at least the minimum bet, and from that point on if you want to bet a sky-high stack of chips, it's fine by them.

Most Roulette tables in Nevada and New Jersey casinos will be at the $1 minimum value. Several casinos will also offer the fifty-cent version, and a few even a twenty-five-cent minimum. You must remember that winning amounts are calculated based on a $1 bet. So, if the value of your chips is fifty cents, any win you get will be half the total value of the amount you would have won if you had bet the $1 standard. For twenty-five-cent chips this will be a quarter of that value.

Since Roulette chips don't have their value printed on them, the dealer tells them apart by colors. If there were three players at the table in addition to you and all bought in for $20 worth of $1 chips, the dealer wouldn't be able to tell them apart if they were all one color. One-dollar chips used in the other table games in the casino are all the same color, usually cream or off-white. If all the four players at this Roulette table had them, neither the dealer nor the players themselves for that matter, would be able to tell who had won.

In this example, you can receive your chips in, say, blue, the second player in yellow, the third in brown, and the fourth player in green. That tells you apart. The colors themselves do not matter. If you win, your color will designate *you* as the winner, and you will be paid with chips of the same color. As long as you play at this same table, the color designated to you will be yours.

Bets in Roulette can be made in a variety of ways and

are generally divided into two groups: "inside" and "outside." Inside bets are any bets made inside the numbered grid on the layout, and outside bets are those made outside the grid. For example, a bet on the number 10 will be an inside bet, while a bet on red will be an outside bet. The basic differences between inside and outside bets lie in how much you can bet and how much you can win. Table limits for inside bets are, generally, $1 minimum and $100 maximum straight up on any single number and up to $2,500 in overall spread, while limits on the outside bets are generally $5 minimum and $5,000 or more maximum. Inside bets pay more, but are harder to win on. Outside bets pay less but win more frequently.

Roulette provides the House with a steady 5.3 percent edge over the player. This edge is constant on all bets at every spin of the wheel. It can be so constant because each new spin of the Roulette wheel is a new event. Neither the wheel nor the ball remembers any past events, and therefore Roulette is among the very few games that allows for such steady House wins. This House edge is derived from the use of the 0 and 00 House numbers; since there are 38 total numbers which can become the winning number, but any such single straight up win will only pay off 35:1, it is pretty clear how this comes about.

This is different in European Roulette, which employs only the single 0; in that game the House edge is only 2.7 percent overall (more on this a little further on in this chapter). Players at Roulette, unlike those at other table games, have no opportunity to reduce this House advantage. Players at Craps, for example, can take full odds on some of their bets, and reduce the House edge by doing so; same for players at Blackjack who play Basic Strategy or count cards. But although this information is quite important to the game aficionado, for casual play it really makes little difference.

Nevertheless, it is important to know what you're giving up when you approach Roulette, and even more so to know the odds against you; this, however, shouldn't deter you from playing Roulette, since, as we will see shortly, there are indeed some bets that can be very profitable in the short term.

♦| INSIDE BETS |♦

The simplest inside bet you can make is a bet on a single number. This is known as a "straight up" bet. This means you place whatever amount you want to bet on one number from among the 38 numbers available (1 through 36, plus the zero and double zero) on the layout grid. You can make this bet after the previous game is over and after the croupier has paid off winners and cleared the table of losing bets, and you can continue to make bets until the croupier calls, "No more bets."

If you make such a single straight up bet, you are wagering that when the ball drops onto the spinning wheel and comes to rest in one of the numbered pockets, it will do so in the specific pocket bearing the number you bet on. If it does, you will be paid 35:1.

Be careful which Roulette table you select. All Roulette tables have a small sign that outlines the betting minimum and maximum for inside and outside bets. But some tables will have a sign that also states the minimum "spread" required for inside bets. Although the table minimum for inside bets may be listed as $1, when you are at a table that requires a minimum spread, you must bet a certain amount in total on the inside, usually $5—that is, five $1 chips spread over the inside grid, or stacked over any single bet option.

Of course, on any Roulette table, you are free to make as many straight up bets as you wish. Needless to say, if you make more than one straight up bet on single numbers, only one of your bets can win; but when it does win it more than makes up for the other bets that lost. (Naturally, if you bet all the 38 numbers you'd be an automatic loser, since the most you can win is 35:1 on any one such bet.)

Instead of betting straight up on any single number, you can also bet on a combination of any two numbers next to each other on the table layout. This is known as a "split," or group-2 bet.

For example, let's say you are at a $1 minimum table without a minimum spread requirement, and you wish to bet the 10 and the 11, but you don't want to bet the full $1 on each number. You do this by placing your $1 chip across the grid line dividing the two numbers you wish to bet on, so that half of your chip peeks out over one of the two numbers, and the other half over the other. This is called "splitting." It tells the croupier that you are betting both numbers with this single bet. You win if either of the two numbers you selected hits. However, instead of getting paid 35:1, as you would on a single number bet, in this case you only get paid 17:1. By increasing your odds of hitting a winner, you directly reduce the payoff on your win.

◆| GROUP BETS |◆

In addition to straight up inside bets, you can also make other inside bets by grouping your numbers. This can be done in a variety of ways. Splitting is one way. But you can also bet any combination of four numbers. To do this, you place your bet on the table layout at a point where the corners of four numbers meet.

Such a bet can be made on any four numbers that form a square on the table layout, like the numbers 10, 11, 13, and 14. To cover these four numbers with a single $1 bet all you have to do is place your $1 bet directly in the center of that square. Again, you increase your chances of winning, but your payoff drops to 8:1 per bet. These so-called "quad" bets (also known as group-4 bets) are, however, advantageous, since you can cover many numbers with a minimum cash outlay and still provide yourself with a profitable win.

Let's say, for example, that you make quad bets on a $1 minimum table, with a $5 minimum spread requirement. You can now cover five times four numbers, $1 on each group of four, for a total of twenty numbers. With a wager like this you can at best expect only an $8 return for your $5 bet if any one of the numbers covered by your five quad bets hits, but you still make a total of $3 in profit; also, you get to keep the $1 that you bet on the quad that won.

This is not a bad way to play Roulette, especially since you can also double-group such quad bets. That is, you can quad the 10, 11, 13, and 14, and also the 7, 8, 10, and 11. In this way the 10 and the 11 ride on both quads. If either 10 or 11 hits, you win your bet twice. You can also progress to a group of six numbers in a similar manner. This is known in Roulette as a "line bet" (not to be confused with the line bet in Craps).

By placing your bet at the T-intersection point on the layout, on the line closest to you that divides any two rows of three numbers, you can cover the group of these six numbers, such as: 7, 8, 9, 10, 11, and 12. The T-intersection point on the bet in this example would be on the grid line closest to where you are sitting and across the line dividing the numbers 7 and 10. The payoff is 5:1 if any of the six numbers picked is hit. Again, this can be done for any combination of six numbers, as long as these numbers are adjacent on the table layout.

Perhaps the most popular group bet, aside from the quad bet, is the row of three. To bet a row of three—say, 13, 14, and 15—you place your bet at the edge of the numbers grid, halfway across the line of the number 13, which is nearest you, without your chips touching any of the lines delineating the neighboring numbers. In other words, your chips will be sitting halfway between the number 13 and the second 12 area, on the line dividing these two betting areas. These so-called group-3 bets can be made on any such row of three numbers. They pay 11:1.

On the inside bets, you can also bet the 0 and 00, either straight up or as a group of two—also known as the "House split." In addition to the group-3 bets discussed above, there are also three possible group-3 bets that include the two House numbers.

The most popular is called a "basket bet," in which you place your chips between the 0 and 00 on the line above the adjacent number 2. In so doing you bet all three numbers 0, 00, and 2. You can also bet the combination 0, 1, and 2 or 00, 2, and 3. These bets work the same as any group-3 bet and also pay 11:1.

A curiosity of Roulette is the group-5 bet. There is only one possible way to do it, and that is to place your chip on the corner of the 0 and 1, to cover the five numbers 0, 00, 1, 2, and 3. It pays 6:1. Such a bet is not available in European Roulette, which only uses one 0. Making this group-5 bet is not the smartest way to play these numbers. Oddswise, you'd be better off betting any of the splits or group-3 bets, or placing all these five numbers straight up.

•| BETTING "0" AND "00" |•

Since the game of Roulette allows you to bet on the House numbers, such bets can be used as safety bets—a kind of insurance. Let's say that you have quite a few bets riding on the inside. If you don't "back" (bet on) the 0 and 00, and the ball lands on either one of them, all your bets lose. It is for this reason that a lot of heavy Roulette players will back the House numbers, either singly or as a split, in proportion to the bets that they have outstanding on the inside.

Practically speaking, however, making this bet is about as valuable as buying insurance in Blackjack. It has little bearing on your overall chances of winning, and you are better served to treat these two House numbers like any other number on the wheel. The probability of either 0 or

00 hitting is exactly the same as that of any of the other numbers.

♦| SEQUENTIAL BETS |♦

Since all inside bets are bets on numbers, or groups of numbers, inside the layout grid, it is important to note that the number arrangement on the layout grid is *sequential*, but that the corresponding numbers on the Roulette wheel are *not* sequentially arranged. This is especially important when applied to group bets. Although, as mentioned earlier, group bets are of advantage to the player, any group bet made on the table layout does not correspond to a like group on the Roulette wheel. For example, a group-4 bet on 10, 11, 13, and 14 has these numbers arranged next to each other on the layout; but on the wheel itself the number 10 is between 25 and 27, the number 11 between 7 and 30, the number 13 between 1 and 36 and the number 14 is between 2 and 35—spread all across the wheel virtually opposite each other. To make a group-4 bet on numbers directly next to each other on the wheel, you would have to place four individual bets on four separate numbers in widely different positions on the table layout—for example, 23, 4, 16, and 33—which defeats the benefit of making group-4 bets.

The number arrangements as they appear on the table layout and on the wheel are not accidental. Oddsmakers who establish the odds and payoffs on Roulette bets know that players will win far more often if allowed to group bets in sequences that represent sequential numbers as they appear on the Roulette wheel. This is not because the mathematics is different, but because in the real world of actual play short-term trends do often appear in direct defiance of laws of mathematical probability. It is, therefore, conceivable that certain groups of numbers—as they appear on the wheel—may, in fact, come up more often than others, even in long streaks. In addition, if the Roulette table is even the tiniest bit off balance—the biased wheel I mentioned earlier—smart players who spot this would clean up by making such group bets.

The table layout therefore gives the *illusion* of sequentiality, while the reality is that the numbers are scattered. Of course, you can still make such bets, but this requires that you make several straight up bets all over the table layout, and cannot, therefore, double up and cross-bet any of your groups. In recent years, however, as part of an attempt to revitalize Roulette play in major casinos, several casinos have introduced a secondary table layout that lists numbers in the sequences in which they actually appear on the wheel.

Such an additional layout is smaller than the traditional one and appears on the table just above the traditional layout on the side where the croupier stands. At first glance, this innovation seems like a good bet for the player, but on closer examination it proves not to be the case.

First, casinos that offer this option often have it only on games with high betting requirements; second, even on such tables the betting requirement for this option is even higher than the already high limits imposed on bets on the traditional layout; and, third, players are only permitted to bet a maximum of five numbers for any one bet.

Again, these limits and rules make such bets unfavorable because players still cannot cross-bet their groups, and, when the dollars are added, they wind up spending more money than if they had made the five bets as straight up inside bets on the traditional layout. This new innovation, therefore, offers merely the illusion of what would be a very good series of bets for the players.

• | OUTSIDE BETS | •

"Outside" bets are bets on events other than any bets, or groups of bets, on the numbers 1 through 36, 0, and 00.

On the table layout the betting area for outside bets is the section closest to the players as they sit opposite the main pit. The betting options are as follows:

A. First 12, second 12, and third 12, in squares—pay 2:1. Betting the squares, the first 12 means you are betting the numbers: 1 through 12, inclusive. Betting the second 12 numbers is covering 13 through 24, and the third 12, 25 through 36.

B. First 12, second 12 and third 12, in columns, called "column bets"—also pay 2:1. The betting area for these column bets is at the opposite end of the table layout from the 0 and 00. If you bet the column bet, the first 12 will cover the numbers: 1, 4, 7, 10, 13, 16, 19, 22, 25, 28, 31, and 34. The second 12 will cover 2, 5, 8, 11, 14, 17, 20, 23, 26, 29, 32, and 35, and the third 12 will cover 3, 6, 9, 12, 15, 18, 21, 24, 27, 30, 33, and 36.

These group-12 bets are the only outside bets that pay odds. All the rest are even-money bets.

C. 1 to 18, and 19 to 36. The former is a bet on any of the first 18 numbers, the latter on the second 18. Both pay even money.

D. Even and odd. The former is a bet on all even numbers on the wheel, the latter on all odd numbers. Both pay even money.

E. Red and black. The former is a bet on all numbers

painted red in color on the wheel, the latter on all numbers painted black. Both pay even money.

Betting outside usually allows higher maximum amounts. If the table minimum is, say $5, the maximum inside bet may be a total of $2,500, with a $100 straight up bet cap—meaning you can only put a maximum of $100 on any single number, up to a total of $2,500 on any inside bet combination. However, outside bets will usually have the same table minimum bet requirement, say $5, but will often allow up to double the inside bet maximum, or $5,000, as in our example. This means you can bet up to $5,000 on any outside bet combination, or any single outside bet. Most often these top limits are played by high rollers who frequently bet either the red or the black. As far as odds of winning go, they might as well bet odd or even, or any of the other even-money outside bets. In all cases, players of American Roulette, which employs both the 0 and 00, are giving up a steady House edge percentage of 5.3 percent on each and every spin of the wheel, on all bets, including even-money bets, regardless of what these bets are, or in what amounts.

Although even-money bets are better than the hard-to-hit high-paying straight up inside bets, if you think that by making even-money bets your odds of winning are fifty-fifty, think again. Because American Roulette uses both the 0 and 00, your chance of hitting any even-money bet, like red or black, is only 47 percent, and not 50 percent. European Roulette, which uses only the single 0, offers better odds of 49 percent on such bets, but that is still not fifty-fifty.

♦| SIMPLE STRATEGY |♦

Although it has been popularized in films and fiction, Roulette, as played in America, is almost universally considered by seasoned gamblers as a sucker's game. And there are powerful arguments that can be made to support this view, especially when compared to European Roulette.

As indicated earlier, European Roulette is played with only the single House number, which so dramatically alters the odds in the player's favor that the game enjoys a considerably higher degree of popularity overseas. But lately, in an effort to revitalize the game of Roulette, quite a few major American casinos have begun to offer European Roulette. For anyone contemplating any kind of serious play on Roulette, this is the game I suggest you look for.

The primary disadvantage of European Roulette as offered in American casinos is that it normally requires much higher minimum bets than does standard American Roulette with the 0 and 00. The reasons are obvious; since the casinos are giving up half their advantage, they want bigger bets to offset it. European Roulette tables in U.S. casinos commonly will require a minimum $5 bet, with a minimum $25 spread on the inside, and a minimum $25 bet on the outside.

If you plan to be a serious Roulette player, with a bankroll to match, these limits should not scare you. The favorable odds you are getting can make up for the higher minimum bets. And if you are a high roller, you will probably bet higher than the minimum anyway, so why play the less favorable 0 and 00 wheel?

There are so many systems to beat the Roulette wheel floating about that just to describe them would require a whole new book. And there are just as many players floating about who have gone broke trying to prove their validity. The fact is, no matter how conservatively you play, the casino advantage will eat you up in the long term. If you played American Roulette for a whole year, twenty-four hours a day, and made even-money bets, in the end you'd still be 5.3 percent short of what you started with.

In Roulette, each new spin is a new event. The wheel and the ball have no memory, and therefore any probability theory based on forecasting future events based on past events is bogus. There is simply no way of telling what the outcome of the next spin will be, based on what past outcomes have been. So, you ask, why should I play Roulette at all? The answer lies in short-term trends.

A "short-term trend" is a description given to any series of regular events that occurs in defiance of expected probability. For example, mathematical probability dictates that if you toss a coin in the air, say, a million times, the outcomes for heads and tails will be equal (to be precise, either heads or tails will appear about 49.99 percent overall). As you toss the coin, however, you may see a series of tosses where the coin will continually land on, say, heads. This is a short-term trend.

In the end, the relative frequency of heads and tails will equate to their expected overall probability, but in the meantime the series of occurrences of heads represents some high variances in frequency outcomes relative to the overall expectations. Simply put, tossing twenty heads in a row represents a massive swing in favor of that event, quite in defiance of the overall expected probability of a "head" event occurring. Applied to Roulette, this means that, on occasion, some number, numbers, groups of numbers, or outside bet events will occur more frequently than others over a period of several spins of the wheel.

Once I watched a game of Roulette at Caesars Palace in Las Vegas, and saw a sequence of twenty-two consecutive winners on red. This was such a short-term trend, very much worth betting into. On another occasion I had an observation session at the Rio in Las Vegas. On this particular table, out of twenty spins, the 0 and 00, considered jointly, came up 9 times. Two players at that table recognized this trend and pressed their bets on the 0 and 00 split. Even though they lost several spins in a row, they more than made up for it when their numbers hit. I do not recommend that you favor any one number over the other, but spotting such short-term trends is the only real advantage players at Roulette have.

The same strategy would apply if you spotted a biased wheel. Since all major gaming centers regularly check the accuracy of their games, such occurrences are rare and do not last long. Perhaps this particular wheel was bumped, or perhaps the wood had settled or reacted to atmospheric changes.

Whatever the case, if you see that the wheel you are playing is hitting a specific area and specific numbers contrary to normal probability, you have either spotted a short-term trend or are playing a biased wheel. In that case the smart Roulette player will alter his betting strategy and bet into this trend or bet into the biased area.

A lot of people employ a betting strategy known as the "double up" system, also known as the "Martingale system." This simple system calls for a player to double his bet each time he loses. The theory goes that, no matter what the short-term trend, eventually that player will hit a winner and recover all his bets, plus the profit of his original betting unit.

This is a far less intelligent betting strategy than it would seem. For example, it would not be unusual to see a player using this system betting $50,000 to win $5, with the $5 being his original even-money bet. Sounds ridiculous? It is. Especially since in any casino you will soon be up against the table limit.

Casinos employ table limits just for this purpose. If they had no table limits, players using the Martingale system, or any of its derivatives, would keep betting till they won. And they would, because, theoretically, whatever bet they made would eventually come up.

But in the real world of casino play this will never be possible. Most casinos will not allow you an open-ended no-limit table. Some casinos will offer their special high rollers private games with very high limits, and other casinos will even take any bet, no matter how big, but the trick is that you have to bet that high amount on the first bet. So you will never get the chance of pushing your bet, as in the double-up system strategy.

Here's the fallacy of any of these so-called double-up systems: Let's say Vasili is playing Roulette in one of the major casinos in America. He is playing on a table with a $5 minimum bet requirement, and a $500 table limit on outside bets. Vasili wants to play the double-up system, so he bets $5 on red. When he loses, he bets $10. A loss means he bets $20 the next time; and $40 after the next loss, $80 after the next, $160 after the next, and so on. After just seven losses in a row, poor Vasili runs up against the table limit. His next bet, the eighth, should be $640, but the table limit is $500. So, even if he bets the limit—$500—on the ninth spin and wins, he wins only $500, for a total gross of $1,000 when his $500 bet—which he gets to keep—is added to his winnings, and all for a net loss of $135! For that sequence of nine bets, Vasili bet a total of $1,135 for a net win of $1,000. A sequence of eight losses in a row on any Roulette bet is not uncommon.

For this reason, betting systems such as these are not merely ludicrous but guarantee that you will lose. If you play this way the casinos will love you, because they know that no matter how much you bet, you are always losing. But an observant player *can* use a betting progression to increase his or her short-term win potential by betting into an existing short-term trend.

If you are such an observant player, and, for example, you were at the same table as Vasili, you would have noticed a short-term trend on black. While Vasili was sweating it out with his progression bets on red, you would have made great profits betting the 8-deep streak of black. In Roulette a series of black hits in a row, or red, or even, or odd, or even a series of specific numbers, happens quite often. And, if you recognize it, betting such short-term trends by increasing your bets after each win works to your advantage. However, unlike the Martingale systems, here you are increasing your bets *when you are winning*, and *not* when you are losing. Simply put, this means you are not chasing your money. In Roulette there are no betting systems that will provide a consistent player advantage for the long term. If you read something to the contrary in magazines or books, you are reading hype and not fact. Nevertheless, some bets in Roulette are better than others and offer player advantages as far as the length of any recognized short-term trend will allow.

To win consistently in Roulette requires luck; but, as in other gambling games, there are some hints I can offer that may help you to win, and certainly reduce your overall losses.

1. Play the European single-zero Roulette if you can find it, because the overall House edge of only 2.7 percent is so much better than the 5.3 percent on American Roulette.

2. Bet splits instead of straight up numbers. This will allow you to cover two numbers with just a single bet. Yes, the payoff is 17:1 and not 35:1 as it is on any single straight up number, but the trick to winning in Roulette is not in maximizing your potential wins but in minimizing your certain losses. Splits are a betting option that allows you to make just one bet, but have two chances at winning it. Anyway, the 17:1 odds are still pretty good, and you can cross-bet your splits, giving yourself even more chances to win while limiting your losses. The fewer dollars you have to bet, the better.

3. Never bet just straight up numbers alone. The odds of winning on any one straight up number are just too long. Instead bet any straight up number with splits to each side of it. For example: Straight up on 11, and splits on: 11 and 8, 11 and 14, 11 and 10, and 11 and 12. Your 11 is the common number, and if it hits you get paid 35:1 on the 11, and 17:1 on the other four splits that had the 11 as the common number. And, of course, if the 11 does not hit, but any of the other numbers you split it with do, you still get 17:1.

4. Bet group-4 quad bets, and group them together to cross-bet and double up on the common numbers. For example, bet a group-4 of 1, 2, 4, and 5. You can then also bet another group-4 with 2, 3, 5, and 6. This gives you the 2 and the 5 as your common numbers. If they hit, you get paid twice. You can expand this still by betting another group, say 4, 5, 7, and 8. This will then give you a three-way 5 and two-way 4 and 5, as well as the 2 and 5 as the common numbers.

5. Bet the first 12, second 12, or third 12, either in square groups or in columns. Any winner will pay 2:1. Bet any two of these combinations, and if you hit, you make a profit of one unit for each two you bet. For example: you bet $5 each on the first and second 12, leaving the third 12 open, and you hit a winner on the second 12. Your first 12 bet will lose, but your second 12 bet will pay you 2:1, or $10. So, you risked a total of $10, and won $10, but you also get to keep the $5 bet on the second 12 bet that won, so you *grossed* $15, giving you an overall profit of $5.

6. Offset your groups. That is, group your bets over different areas of the board. If you bet groups at the top of the table layout, also bet a similar group at the other end of the layout. Remember, the wheel

does not have the numbers grouped in the same sequence as they are shown on the table layout. By offsetting your groups, you cover a wider portion of the Roulette wheel.

7. Watch for short-term trends. If you spot one, whatever it is, bet into it immediately and continue to bet into it and press your bets as long as it lasts. But remember that trends can be as brief as two in a row, or as long as fate can make them. Don't push it if it's not there.

8. Remember how much you are betting in your total spread. If the amount of your expected win on any single or combination bet is less than the total amount you bet, you are a loser before the game even begins. So pay attention to the value of your gaming chips, remember how many you bet and where, and calculate what your win potential is before you make the bets.

9. If you win, press your bet, but don't blow it all on the next spin. Try to play with the money you won, and keep the money you bought in with. This way you are likely to feel better about bigger bets and also give yourself a chance to win bigger wins if you hit again. If you lose, go back to your minimum bet and start over again.

10. If you have the money, make the even-money bets in as large amounts as your bankroll can take. Even though any such bets win only 47 percent of the time on American Roulette, the odds of winning on them are still far better than any others at Roulette. In addition, short-term trends appear more frequently and last longer on such even-money outside bets. The player that the House is most afraid of is one who comes to a table, bets the largest amount possible on a bet with the least advantage to the House, and then collects his winnings and leaves.

Time is your enemy, especially in Roulette. The longer you stay and play, the more money the House wins from you, no matter how lucky you are. So, if you are a high roller and you want to play Roulette, play this way. Whatever the amount of your bankroll, play for five minutes on either black or red, or odd or even, betting as much as you can afford, keep an eye out for any short-term trend, and you're likely to win far more than if you stayed there for hours playing straight up numbers for the highest possible payoff of 35:1.

The best advice I can give you for Roulette is the same as for Craps: Get in, make your money, and get out. Any prolonged exposure to the game of Roulette will inevitably lead you to lose money. But if you're smart, observant, and know how to bet into the short-term trends you recognize, you can make as much in a few minutes of play as you could ever hope to make by grinding out small percentages over long periods of time, as dictated by the few poor souls still plugging progressive Roulette systems.

Although it looks complicated, Baccarat—pronounced with the silent "t" —is the simplest card game played in contemporary American casinos. It is played in a separate, closed-off area called the "Baccarat Pit" and on a large table generally seating twelve players.

There are only three bets that players can make in this game, and the result of any hand is entirely governed by a strict set of rules. As played in America, Baccarat is a game of pure chance that requires no skill on the part of the players. This is slightly different from the Baccarat games played in Europe, where players actively participate in the dealing of the cards and in decisions concerning the draw of extra cards.

American Baccarat retains some of the rules of its European counterpart, such as offering the Bank to players in turn, sometimes asking one player to deal the cards and another to turn the cards over, but in essence the game is played by players against the cards, however drawn. The House collects commissions from all players who backed the "Banker's" hand, irrespective of who made such a bet, and also collects all losing bets. I'll explain all this in more detail a little later on.

American casinos intentionally propagate an aura of wealth and sophistication for Baccarat, in a conscious effort to attract high rollers. To some extent they have to, because the small House edge requires that huge sums of money be bet in order for the House to make a decent profit. Nevertheless, of all the games offered in American casinos, Baccarat is by far the best bet for your gaming dollar. Its House edge is so small that any bet in Baccarat provides the player with good odds of winning, offering as little as 1.1 percent edge in the favor of the House—specifically a little more than 1.2 percent on "Player" hands, and 1.1 percent on "Banker" hands.

Yet many people avoid the game entirely. Perhaps this is because of its intimidating aura of sophistication, or its complicated-looking setup, and the high betting limits generally required for play. However, none of these should deter you from playing the game, especially because many casinos now offer Baccarat with lower limits, and even a streamlined version—called Mini-Baccarat—which is played in the main casino. Mini-Baccarat is played on a Blackjack-style table, and its rules are exactly the same as those of the main Baccarat version. The table layout is almost the same but allows for only seven players, as opposed to the full complement of twelve players in the big game.

There are only two other differences between Mini-Baccarat and the pit game: first, Mini-Baccarat generally offers much lower betting limit requirements than does the big game, often as low as $5 per bet, and, second, the game is dealt exclusively by a single dealer in much the same manner as Blackjack. This makes it appear more friendly to the casual player and thereby eliminates the intimidation factor often felt by players who consider the main pit game. Since Mini-Baccarat is also played in the main casino and not in a cordoned-off area, this further eliminates the apparent exclusivity of the game and makes it easier for casual players to try.

Since both Baccarat and Mini-Baccarat are played by exactly the same rules, I will first explain the game as it is played on the large table in the main pit, and then give a few extra pointers about Mini-Baccarat at the end of the chapter.

•| HOW TO RECOGNIZE BACCARAT |•

Baccarat can easily be spotted because it is played on large tables most often located in enclosed areas lavishly decorated with plush seating, chandeliers, and other amenities designed to give this game a feeling of Old World elegance.

The Baccarat table is rectangular in shape and about the size of a Craps table—but flat and not sunken like the Craps table—and has twelve spaces for players, six on each side, numbered 1 through 6 on one side and 7 through 12 on the other. Each player position features three betting areas, marked "Player," "Banker," and "Tie." Toward the top center of the table layout is a series of little boxes also numbered 1 through 12, corresponding to the seat numbers allocated to players. These are the commission boxes, where dealers place the players' appropriate commission payments due the House before each player leaves the game.

Standing in the middle, between players, and facing one another are the casino employees who run the game. On one side are two dealers, one for each six player spots on either side of the long end of the large table. These dealers

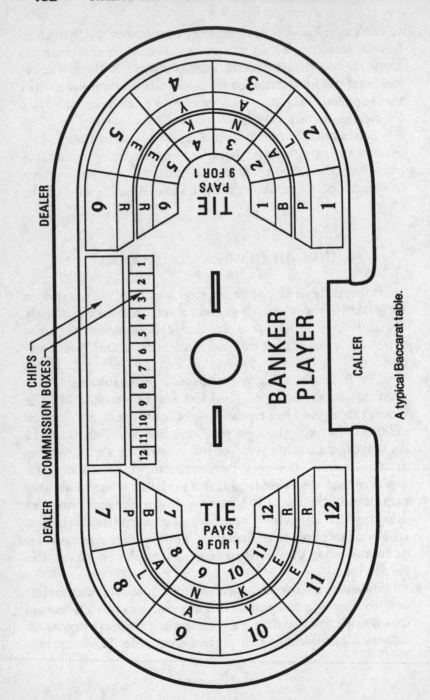

A typical Baccarat table.

handle the money, pay winning bets, take losing bets, and collect and keep track of players' commissions. Across the table opposite the dealers stands the "Caller." The Caller is a man or woman whose job is to announce the values of each hand dealt, somewhat like the Stickman in Craps. This Caller uses an odd-looking elongated paddle to move the cards around the table. Some large casinos with lots of Baccarat action employ two callers, one to handle the cards with this paddle and the other to arrange them in the center of the table and call out their values.

◆| **HOW THE GAME IS PLAYED** |◆

As with all table games, you begin by changing your cash money into gaming chips. In Baccarat, these gaming chips are quite a bit bigger than the regular casino chips. There is absolutely no reason for this other than the aura of special importance that Baccarat seeks to cultivate. Perhaps the casinos think that players will feel better about betting large amounts if they have big chips in their hands. But no matter how big these chips are, they function in exactly the same way as any other gaming chips in play throughout the casino. They can be changed for cash if you wish, or for regular casino chips.

At the Baccarat table it doesn't matter which seat you take. Unlike Blackjack, in which position selection can be advantageous in a game with more players, in American Baccarat you are not playing against the other players or against the House. Your betting action is against the cards. It therefore makes no difference what the other players bet on, or how much, or in what order the cards are dealt. In Blackjack, for instance, other players at the table ahead of you in the turn of dealing can affect what cards you will receive when it's your turn to draw, which is why position selection can be so important. But in American Baccarat it doesn't matter.

Even if a designated player at the Baccarat table does draw the cards, no player decisions are involved. Whether any additional cards are drawn depends entirely on the strict set of rules governing the draw of such extra cards. Consequently there is no possibility that a player in the position in front of you will receive the cards you would otherwise have received.

Chances are that if you sit down at a Baccarat table the game will be already in progress. Very rarely are Baccarat tables unoccupied. Many casinos in fact employ House players, called "shills," a couple of whom are often seated at the Baccarat table so that potential customers won't have to be the first to sit down or play alone. The shills are paid employees of the casino, and they play with House money; they don't get to keep any winnings, but they don't lose either. Shills in Baccarat are just there to occupy seats. When a sufficient number of customers arrive, the House players leave, returning only if the table becomes empty again. Unlike in Poker, Baccarat shills have no effect on your hands. If, however, you feel uncomfortable about knowing whether or not there are any shills at the table, just ask the casino Pit Boss if there are any at your table. By law, casinos must identify shills if asked.

Baccarat is played with eight standard decks of cards, no jokers, all shuffled together. When the game is at the point of a new shuffle—either at the very beginning or when the cards dealt have reached the cut card, as in Blackjack—one of the dealers will call out, "Shuffle," and begin to shuffle the cards. When the shuffle is completed, one of the customers will be asked to cut the deck and the cut decks will then be placed in the shoe, ready for dealing. At this point one of the dealers, usually the one who did the shuffle, will turn up the first card out. Whatever the value of this first card, it indicates how many cards will be burned. If, for example, the first card out is 6, the dealer will burn six cards, none of which the players see, placing them in the discard tray along with that first card out. The game is now ready to be played.

The shoe containing the eight shuffled decks is called "the Bank." It is so called because in European games the person holding it actually has to back all the bets and therefore really is the banker. This is not the case in American Baccarat. In American Baccarat, the player holding the bank has no specific advantage over other players.

The player holding the bank does not win any more money, does not have to bet on the Bank hand, is not responsible for paying winning bets, makes no choices affecting the draw of extra cards, and will not collect any losing bets. This action is merely a cosmetic copy of the European version of Baccarat.

Unlike in European Baccarat, where players can play for or buy the Bank, in American Baccarat the Bank is simply given to the player seated immediately to the right of the dealer (position 7) at the beginning of the new game. Each player at the table is then given the Bank in turn and can hold it as long as the Bank wins. Once it loses, the Bank moves to the player on his or her right, counterclockwise, and so on.

Before any cards are dealt, all players at the table make their bets—to be explained shortly—and dealing takes place. The player holding the Bank deals out four cards, two sets of two cards, with the first and third cards going to the official Player's hand, and the second and fourth cards to the Banker's hand. The Banker's hand cards are tucked under the side of the shoe by the player who holds the Bank and is dealing, while the Player's hand cards are given by the Caller, using that odd paddle, to one of the other players, usually the player who made the biggest bet on the Player's hand.

This designated player then picks up the first two cards, looks at them, and tosses them face up to the Caller, who then arranges them in the center of the table in a special area marked on the table layout as "Player." Now the player who holds the Bank picks up the two Bank hand cards he had tucked under the side of the shoe, looks at them, and also tosses them over to the Caller, who arranges them in that same special area in the center of the table marked on the layout as "Banker." This area is directly above the one marked "Player." Again, remember that these two areas are separate from the betting areas, also so named; they are located in the center of the table layout and are used only to distinguish which cards have been dealt to which hand.

Although these moves in Baccarat make the game seem complicated, I wish to point out one more time that they are really quite unnecessary and have absolutely no effect on the outcome of the game. They are just a relic from European Baccarat, in which the Banker and the Player in fact *do* control the cards and decisions for drawing cards and standing. Not so in this American version, where the hand's final values would be exactly the same even if none of these moves were made by the players but were simply dealt by the dealer.

Players can make bets at the conclusion of any hand or after a new shuffle. There are only three betting areas available, each clearly marked and displayed on the table layout in front of each player position. These are bets on the Bank hand; on the Player hand; or on the Tie hand. To make any one such bet, you place your gaming chips in the area so marked. You can make any one, two, or all three bets at the same time, but to bet all three is to automatically lose at least one hand, and more often than not two hands, and is therefore not a good idea.

♦| VALUE OF HANDS AND RULES |♦

For the bettor, the object of Baccarat is to place a wager on the hand that will, at the close of dealing, be closest to 9 in total value, without going over. On this most basic level, it bears some resemblance to Blackjack. The differences between these two games, however, are far greater than their similarities.

First of all, in Baccarat the value of cards is calculated differently than in Blackjack, as well as in most other card games. In Baccarat, all 10-value cards and face cards are counted as zero, aces are counted as 1, and all other cards are counted at their numerical value. (The various suits—hearts, diamonds, clubs, and spades—play no role in this game.) If, then, either Baccarat hand has a king and a 2, the value of the hand is 2.

Second, there are very strict rules dictating whether, after the first two cards dealt, more are to be drawn—rules based on the total value of this initial set of two cards dealt to each hand. Third, players in Baccarat have no choice in what cards are drawn and cannot manipulate the outcome. Fourth, there are no individual hands dealt to players. Fifth, the game eventually ends on its own and bets are paid purely on this final result. Winning, therefore, depends on what betting option you placed your bet on.

The rules for drawing extra cards are somewhat different for Banker hands and Player hands. After the first two cards are dealt to both the Player and the Banker hands, whether further cards are drawn depends on what the two-card total for the Player hand is. First action, therefore, takes place on the Player hand. If the Player hand has an original two-card total of 0, 1, 2, 3, 4, or 5, a third card must be drawn to the Player hand. If the original two-card value is 6 or 7, the Player hand must stand. The rules concerning the Banker hand are a little different and depend on what the Player hand total is, with two exceptions.

These exceptions are: When the Banker hand has an original two-card value of 0, 1, or 2, the Banker hand must draw a third card; and the Banker hand stands if it had an original two-card value of 7. The remaining rules for Banker hands depend on what the Player hand results are.

If the Player hand stands, the Banker hand draws a third card only if it had an original two-card value of 3, 4, or 5. If the Player hand draws a third card, and the Banker hand original two-card total is 3, the Banker hand draws a third card only if the Player hand had drawn a total of 0, 1, 2, 3, 4, 5, 6, or 9. The Banker hand, therefore, stands if the Player hand had drawn to an 8. If the Player hand draws a third card, and the Banker hand had an original two-card value of 4, the Banker hand draws a third card only if the Player hand had drawn 2, 3, 4, 5, 6, or 7, and stands otherwise. And, under the same conditions, if the Banker hand has a 5, it will draw a third card only if the Player hand had drawn 4, 5, 6, or 7, and stands otherwise. If the Banker hand has a 6, it will draw a third card only if the Player hand had drawn 6 or 7, and, again, stands otherwise. If either the Player hand or the Banker hand is dealt an 8 or 9 on the first two cards, this is called a "natural." To receive a natural is the desired objective in Baccarat. If this total is so dealt to either hand, or both, that hand must stand and no further action is taken.

A natural is an automatic winner to the hand that draws it, unless the other hand has a higher natural or both hands have the same natural. If, for example, the Player hand draws a natural 9, and the Banker hand draws a natural 8, both must stand, but the Player hand wins with the higher natural. Of course, the reverse is also true. In cases where both the Player hand and the Banker hand draw the same natural, say 9, it is called a "tie." Neither hand wins or loses, but the payoff is made on those bets placed on the tied hand.

Tied hands do not occur frequently, but when they do, they do not necessarily have to occur on naturals. Even though the rules for drawing and standing are quite complex and depend on what events occur when cards are dealt, sometimes both hands wind up tied. It is only on these occasions that Baccarat players are paid odds—that is, better than even money. Tied hands pay off at 9:1, while the other two bets, Banker and Player hands, only pay off at even money.

I know that these rules may sound somewhat confusing, but even if you do not memorize them all it will not affect your success one bit. In all games of American Baccarat, it is the casino dealers who call for the draw of the cards or draw the cards themselves, so you don't have to be concerned with intimate details of the game or worry about what cards will be drawn or whether you should ask for a draw. The information I supplied here will make it clearer why the game plays out the way it does, but the ultimate outcome depends on the cards alone and not you. It is your bet that will determine if you win and how much you win.

♦| HOW TO BET |♦

There are only three betting options in modern American Baccarat: a bet on the Player hand, a bet on the Banker hand, and a bet on the tied hand.

To bet on the Player hand is to bet that the cards drawn for the Player will have a total value, at the end of all dealing and drawing, greater than that of the Banker hand. To make this bet, you place your gaming chips in the area marked "Player" in front of you. You can bet any amount from the table minimum up to the table maximum.

If, after the hand has ended the Player hand wins, you win even money. For example, if the Player hand draws, say, king-2-4, and the Banker hand draws 3-jack-ace, Player hand wins. Player hand total is 6, and Banker hand total is 4. When the Player hand wins, all other bets lose.

To bet on the Banker hand, by contrast, is to bet that at the end of the hand the Banker hand is the winner, and all other bets lose. To make this bet, you place your gaming chips in the area in front of you marked "Banker." As with the bet on the Player hand, in this case as well you will be paid even money if you win. You will, however, be charged a standard 5 percent commission on the amount of your win.

This commission, known as "vigorish" (or "vig," for short) is charged only on winning bets made on the Banker hand, but is not immediately deducted from your winnings. It will instead be placed by the dealer in the commission grid on the table layout in the box whose number corresponds to the number of your position at the table. This indicates that you owe the House that amount. You can settle this commission at any time, but you *must* always settle it if you get up to leave the table.

The dealer uses House chips and actual coins to denote the amount of the commission you owe the House. Because commissions can run in fractions, casinos use quarters, half-dollars, and silver dollars in addition to regular casino gaming chips to progressively account for the amount of commissions you owe, for as long as you are playing. The reason the House charges this commission on bets on the Banker hand is because the odds slightly favor such bets. The House edge is 1.2 percent on Player hands, but only 1.1 percent on the Banker hands. This small fraction is enough to account for a few more winners, overall, on Banker hands than on Player hands. Because of this small House edge in Baccarat, the House needs to charge such commissions in order to make more money from the game than would be allowed merely by that overall House edge. Combined, these jointly provide the House with steady, forecastable profits.

Some casinos will offer lower commissions on Banker hands in big game Baccarat in an effort to attract more high rollers. Often you will see advertisements in major casinos for 4 percent commission, and occasionally a commission even as low as 2 percent. This makes those Baccarat games more attractive to players who bet large amounts, but for casual players it makes little difference in the short term.

A few years ago I remember hearing a story about a famous Baccarat player and his experiences in Atlantic City. This player was known the world over for his Baccarat play. For him it was not unusual to bet a cool quarter million on any one hand. With bets as large as these, it is no wonder that such bettors are attracted to games offering a low vig. On this particular occasion he had just arrived from Australia, where he had won $26 million at Baccarat. In Atlantic City he quickly lost $16 million and wanted more credit.

The casino said no, and the player was furious. He locked himself in his suite and refused to leave until he was given more credit. Finally the casino owner was called and gave this player another $6 million in credit. He promptly lost it, and demanded $3 million more. He was refused and vowed never to return to that casino again. At this threat, the casino gave him another $3 million in credit. Perhaps they shouldn't have, because he won $16 million and left.

It is big gamblers like these who are most affected by what the percentage of the House vig is. If, for example, such a high roller bet $200,000 on the Bank hand and won, at a 5 percent vig he would pay the House $10,000. This is a large amount to just give away.

But at a 4 percent vig, this commission would have been only $8,000; the saving of $2,000 per hand is quite large, especially so when you consider that Baccarat players bet, on average, around thirty to forty hands per hour. However, for the casual player, even if you play a Baccarat game with the 5 percent vig, and consistently bet on the Banker hand and win, the overall amount of commission for the time you spend at the game will not add up to enough to warrant passing up this table in favor of a game offering a 4 percent vig. In any case, these lower vig games often have high minimum bet requirements, and this puts them out of reach of most casual players.

♦| TIED HAND |♦

To bet on a tied hand means to bet that both the Player hand and the Banker hand will have the same total value after all cards for this hand are drawn. To make this bet, you place your wager in the area in front of you marked "Tie," and into the box whose number corresponds to the table position you occupy. You can also simply toss the money you wish to bet into the center of the table and call out to the dealer that you want this placed on the tied hand. The dealer will then put it in the right spot for you. If a tied hand is drawn, your bet will be paid at 9:1 and no vig is charged.

Betting the tie is basically a side bet in Baccarat. It sounds like a good deal, but it should be mentioned that tied hands in Baccarat are quite rare. This is because the rules for hitting and standing tend to break up possible ties. And with eight decks all shuffled together, the chances that the flow of any four or more cards dealt at random will have an ultimate total value that is equal, as counted by Baccarat rules, are slim indeed.

Nevertheless, a bet on tie can provide, on occasion, a substantial win. Since this is the only bet that pays odds in Baccarat, it should be exploited either as an occasional side bet made in addition to a bet on either the Player or Banker hand, or when you spot a short-term trend toward possible ties. As with all gambling games, your observation skills and timely choices can allow you to catch one of those rare streaks that happen in all gambling games, as I mentioned in several previous chapters.

♦| KEEPING SCORE |♦

When you sit down at a Baccarat game you will most likely be given a pencil and a chart. The chart has a line grid on which you can mark the results of the hands you play, whether the Bank hand wins, or the Player, or if there is a tie. This card is offered because Baccarat players like to keep track of trends in hands, which is a good idea.

This simple tool does not affect the game, but it can provide you with information on short-term trends. After a few hands you will be able to see which hands are winning more frequently than others, and you can use this information to tailor your betting strategy. I have said several times that short-term trends are the key to winning. This is especially so in Baccarat. Cards, no matter how they are shuffled, often tend to run in groups. These groupings can translate into winning trends for Banker or Player hands in Baccarat with almost startling frequency.

The scorecard is sometimes considered to be just another gimmick that casinos use to cater to the big players, but it can provide the casual player with the same advantages as high rollers. Keeping score like this will not, of course, guarantee that you'll win. Indeed, the very fact that casinos offer it should tell you something about its potential success rate. If this were a surefire trick for winning, it would most likely be banned by the casinos rather than freely offered. Nonetheless, it can offer a guide to short-term trends, and *any* form of assistance in determining likely trends is welcome and should be used to its full advantage.

◆ | MINI-BACCARAT | ◆

Although it does not have all the glamour associated with its posh cousin, Mini-Baccarat is perhaps the game more suited to the casual gambler seeking a good game, favorable odds, and a friendly atmosphere. It is the same game as that found in main pit Baccarat and offers the same good odds but without the pomposity and rigmarole.

Mini-Baccarat is played on a Blackjack-size table with seven player spots and single dealer doing all the dealing. It has none of the needless ceremony surrounding who deals the cards, who holds the Bank, and so on. All the rules, betting options, as well as the vig, are exactly the same as those used in main pit Baccarat. The only differences are in the table layout, how the dealing takes place, where the cards dealt are arranged, and how many players can sit at the table.

At the Mini-Baccarat table, each player spot has two circles, one above the other, in front of his position. The one closest to the player is labeled "Player" and the one above it is labeled "Banker." Above it is a semicircular strip about two inches wide running the length of the table, labeled "Tie" at either end, and divided into numbered areas which directly correspond to the players' positions at the table.

Directly in front of the dealer is the chip tray where all House gaming chips are kept, and directly in front of it is the commission box grid. Eight decks of cards are used, just as in the main pit Baccarat game.

The single dealer—dressed in casino uniform, not a tuxedo—does all the shuffling; a player selected by the dealer cuts the cards after each shuffle; the shuffled and cut decks are placed in the shoe; one card is dealt face up and other cards subsequently burned (depending on the value of that

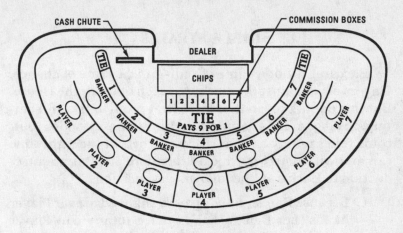

The Mini-Baccarat table.

first card)—again the same as in the main pit Baccarat game; bets are made by the players and the hand begins. The dealer deals the first and third card to his or her right, and the second and fourth card to the left. Usually there are no designated areas on the table layout for Mini-Baccarat marked as Banker and Player into which these cards are dealt, as in the main pit Baccarat game. But this doesn't matter. The hand dealt to the dealer's right is always the Player hand, and the other is always the Banker hand. In all other respects the game plays the same as its rich cousin in the main pit.

The advantages of Mini-Baccarat for the casual player are the generally low betting requirements—usually starting with a $5 minimum bet and with a $500 maximum bet per hand, and the casual atmosphere, in addition to the good odds the game offers.

Another advantage is that Mini-Baccarat tables often have very few players, which gives the dealer time to explain any nuances of the game that you may wish to ask about. It is, therefore, a good introduction to Baccarat.

◆| SIMPLE STRATEGY |◆

Baccarat is not a game of skill—it is a game of chance. Players play against the cards, not each other or the House. But this doesn't mean that there isn't room for skillful betting. In all gambling games, even those whose win/loss outcome relies purely on chance, proper bets at the right time can and will assist your luck. I therefore offer, as an introduction to Baccarat, the following suggestions:

1. Because Banker hands have a slight edge over Player hands, bet Banker hands twice to any one Player hand bet, *unless* you have spotted a certain trend in favor of Player hands.

2. Bet into any short-term trend you see, but be ready to alternate your Player hand and Banker hand bets. Trends change, and can be as short as two hands, or as long as ten hands in a row, or even longer. (Keep track of the game and trends with the chart card; if you are not offered one, ask for it.)

3. Bet the tie hand occasionally, especially if you see that the flow of cards has brought some near-ties, but without hitting one for some time.

4. As always, bet the table minimum when you begin. If you win, play with the money you won. If you win again, press your bet by one chip each time you win. If you lose, go back to the table minimum. The idea is to play with the House money as much as possible and to bet into winning streaks, not losing ones.

These simple suggestions are by no means the be-all and end-all of strategy play, but they will provide for a better approach to the game for anyone not familiar with Baccarat, or for players looking to find a basic framework upon which to base betting decisions.

♥ ♦

8
CASINO POKER

♣ ♠

One of my favorite Poker stories is the one where during the taping of a television commercial Bobby Berosini and his orangutans—popular headliners on the Las Vegas stage—are casually seated at a Poker table, playing cards and drinking beer. On one such occasion, late at night, a slightly tipsy patron walked by, took a scared look at this table, then turned to his wife and was overheard remarking: "Honey, let's go home; when I start seeing apes playing Poker I *know* it's time to go."

Of all the games offered in the modern casino, Poker is perhaps the best known, rivaled only by Blackjack. But unlike Blackjack, Poker is also greatly misunderstood by the casual casino patron. Probably most of us have played Poker at some time or another, and most of us likely think we are pretty familiar with how the game works. However, the Poker played in modern casino resorts is often quite unlike the game we played on Poker night at home.

The atmosphere of modern casino Poker—with its large rooms and many tables, crowds of people, players coming in and out of games in progress, betting limits, complicated strategies, flashing lights, distractions caused by cocktail service and staff movements, plus the constant 24-hour action—makes this game considerably different from the kitchen-table game at home.

True, much of what you will encounter in casino Poker may already be familiar, but the peculiarities found in all aspects of the casino Poker experience may not be. Casino Poker is a game of great variety, both in the kind of Poker games offered, but also in how the games are played. The most popular Poker variations are Seven Card Stud and Texas Hold-Em. But other, perhaps lesser-known games, are also offered in great numbers—games like Omaha, Low Ball, High-Low, and still others.

There are many features that set Poker apart from the rest of the casino games. First, Poker is the only game in which the House is merely a spectator, simply providing the game, facilities, and staff for its customers. As a result, players at Poker do not play against the House, but against each other. Second, Poker is also the only casino game that does not have a built-in House edge. Because the House does not participate but merely deals the game, it has no way of manipulating the rules to guarantee its own cut, as it can in all the other games. But the House still needs to make money from Poker; otherwise it would not be able to pay for the facilities and staff necessary to make the game available to its customers. The House therefore charges a commission on the size of each pot. The "pot" is the total amount of money that is bet by all players in a hand of Poker. The pot increases in value with each round of betting, and is won by the player with the best hand at the end of any one game.

The commission the House charges, also known as the "rake," is usually between 2 percent and 10 percent of the pot, and it is progressively deducted from the pot by the dealer as the game goes on.

Third, Poker is more a game of skill than of chance. Yes, chance still plays a part, but winning or losing depends more on the skill employed by players and less on the cards they are dealt. In all other casino card games it is the cards which determine the winner, and players therefore play the cards. In Poker, this is not necessarily so, because players play against other players and can successfully do it with whatever cards they are dealt.

This also means that there are practically no set guidelines for how to play any given set of cards dealt to you. To be sure, there are standard rules for Poker, such as the hierarchy of hands; but within the limitation of these rules the possibilities are almost unlimited. This makes Poker a more volatile game, since a bad hand that is played well can often win against a good hand played badly. And fourth, Poker is the only game where your success depends not merely on what you do, what cards you get, and how you play the game, but also on what the other players do and how they play their hands. In all other casino games you play your hand to win; in Poker, however, it is best to play your *opponent's hand to lose.*

You may have a good hand, but it may not be good enough if another player has a better one. But skill in Poker allows you to play your hand as if it has greater value than it really does. And the only way to do this is to play in a manner that will make the other players *think* that your hand is better than it really is. This is what I mean when I say that in Poker you play your opponent's hand to lose. It is not uncommon to see players with good hands simply drop out if another player with a far inferior hand plays it well enough to make them think their hand cannot win. Such a player won because he played the other player's hand to lose.

Therefore, of all the games offered in a casino, Poker is

the only game which can, when played well, be consistently beaten for profit. Indeed, many professional Poker players make a good living at it. But to play like a professional Poker player requires years of practice, an in-depth understanding of the game, considerable people skills, careful money management, and a lot of patience. These skills and techniques are also important for any casual encounter with casino Poker, but if you approach the game thinking you will make a life-altering win at it, you're wrong and you will be a loser very quickly.

To make thousands at Poker, you must bet thousands and win consistently. To do this you must play the high-end games, and these games are mostly played by Poker players who have been playing Poker for a lifetime, and they will clean you out. This entire book has been directed toward offering some easy-to-understand guidelines for smart play. This chapter is no different, but remember my words of caution. It is true that you can be very lucky; even the clumsiest player can have a run of luck and win. But to rely only on such lucky streaks is to be foolhardy. No matter how lucky you are, luck without skill in Poker equals a fast trip home with an empty billfold.

All that I have said thus far is not intended to scare you off this game. Poker is a fun, rewarding and exciting game to play, even if you know just the very basics. But you must know something beside just the rules regarding which hand beats what.

◆ HOW TO RECOGNIZE CASINO POKER ◆ AND HOW TO BEGIN

There are many different Poker games offered in most casinos, but, as I mentioned, the most popular are Seven Card Stud and Texas Hold-Em games. I will, therefore, confine all further explanations of Poker to these two games when discussing Poker in general, and, a little further on, I will discuss each of these two games individually.

Most, but not all, major casinos set aside a specific area for Poker. It is usually separated from the main casino floor, like Baccarat, and generally carries a large sign over the entrance identifying it. In this area are several Poker tables. Depending on the size of the casino and its interest in offering Poker, this room can have as few as two tables, or as many as the customer demand warrants.

Above each table hangs a sign specifying what variety of Poker is being played there and what the betting limits are. (This same information will also be noted on a plastic card next to the dealer on the table itself.) Tables normally accommodate seven players, although some, particularly in Texas Hold-Em games, can accommodate up to fourteen. Poker tables are not covered with the kind of felt found on Blackjack tables, but instead with a material like vinyl. Cards easily slide on this surface, making dealing easier. There is a House dealer, in uniform, who deals the game from a standard single deck of fifty-two cards. Since the game is played by players against each other, and not against the House, as in Blackjack, the dealer is merely a spectator as far as the outcome of the game is concerned. He does, however, also shuffle, announces the value of cards as they are dealt, compares final hands to determine the winner, handles all the money, changes cash into chips, and generally renders decisions when a dispute occurs.

Sometimes the dispute can involve the dealer, such as when he makes a dealing error, in which case the dealer calls the Poker Room manager to render judgment. The manager's judgment is final, and no appeals can be made. The manager also intervenes in disputes where any player or players complain about the correctness or accuracy of any judgment made by the dealer. Otherwise a casino Poker game is entirely between the players.

In order to join a game, the first thing you must do is walk up to the counter in front of the Poker Room and ask the Poker Room manager, or one of his assistants, if there is a seat available at the game you wish to play in. Often games are full, so the Poker Room manager has a list in which he writes the names of players waiting for a seat. Depending on how full the casino is at the time you arrive, this wait can be as short as a few minutes, and as long as an hour. Generally, however, the wait tends to be shorter, since most casinos have many tables in action during peak periods, and player turnover is high. When an opening becomes available in the game you requested, the Poker Room manager will call out your name, and you will be seated at whatever position is open at that game. Therefore, in a game in progress, you have no choice of which position you'll get. If, however, while you are at the table, another position at that table becomes open, you can request to move into that seat; in that case you are given priority over any new player coming into the game.

The only time you can actually select a specific position at the table is when a new game is started, and you are one of the first players to open the game. Position selection doesn't matter a great deal; its only real advantage is in how well you see the cards on the table. Since Poker tables are large, sitting in the middle, opposite the dealer, is better, because you can then easily see the whole table.

All Poker games are played with Poker gaming chips. The *only* exceptions are games with very high stakes, where cash also plays. However, the overwhelming majority of casino Poker tables play exclusively with chips. The important rule to remember here is: "Cash does not play." Should you, for example, have only $10 in gaming chips left and you wish to raise the next bet by $10 over the $10 in chips that you have, you will not be allowed to do so, even if you have a $20 bill in your pocket or even in full view on the table in front of you.

Poker games generally use standard casino gaming chips. Some casinos have special $1 and fifty-cent gaming chips in use, but for the most part the gaming chips used here are the same as those used in all other table games in that casino. You can therefore play Poker with the same gaming chips with which you play Blackjack or Craps.

When you first sit down at a table, wait till the current hand is completed. If the Poker Room manager has not already provided you with the gaming chips you want, toss your cash into the center of the table and ask the Poker dealer for change. Unless this is one of those rare high-stakes games where cash can be used in play, the dealer will always change all the cash you give him into gaming chips. Stack them up in front of you, and the game is on.

♦| SEVEN CARD STUD |♦

Seven Card Stud is by far the most popular game among casino Poker patrons. Perhaps the reason is the game's apparent simplicity or its close resemblance to the Poker games played at home. The generally lower betting limits also make it attractive to casual players. A standard 52-card deck is used, without jokers, and there are no wild cards. It is played on a table generally seating seven players.

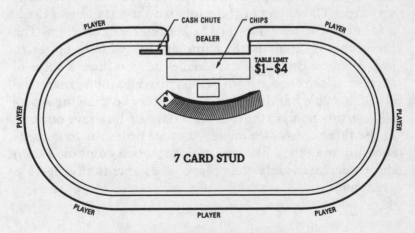

A typical table for Seven Card Stud.

◆│ HOW TO PLAY │◆

The dealer begins the game by dealing cards to all players seated at the table, beginning with the player immediately to the dealer's left, and then continuing clockwise around the table. Seven cards in total will eventually be dealt out to each player.

The first two are dealt face down to all players; only you get to see the first two cards dealt to you, as do each of the other players with their two cards. These are called, appropriately enough, "down cards." Then, in turn, four cards will be dealt face up to each player, one for each round of betting; these cards, called "up cards," are exposed for all players to see. Finally, in the last round, a seventh down card is also dealt to each player. Before any betting takes place, each player will, therefore, receive a total of three cards in the first round—two down cards and one up card.

If you stay in the game through all rounds of betting, at the end you will have three cards face down, which only you can see, and four cards face up, which your opponents can see as well. You, of course, can also see your opponents' up cards. The object of the game is to use the seven cards and make the best five-card Poker hand out of them. The hierarchy of hands is the same as that which applies to Video Poker. But in Seven Card Stud you have a total of seven cards to choose from, which provides for a great variety of possible hands. Some players may be showing a possible strong hand in the four cards face up but have nothing in the three cards face down. At other times the four cards showing may look like garbage, but when combined with the three cards only that player sees eventually make a great hand.

♦| HOW TO BET |♦

Betting in any Poker game involves several moves, including bets before the initial set of cards is dealt, during the course of the current game as further cards are dealt, and at the end when all cards have been dealt and the remaining players in that game battle it out to see who wins.

In most Poker games a small amount of money—usually $1 to $4—is generally required from all players at the start of a hand. It is like buying into the round, or buying your first set of cards, and games that use it do so to make the pot bigger and so assure that the winner will get at least something even if no further bets are made. This is the so-called "ante." In many low-limit Seven Card Stud games this ante is often not required.

Since a lot of this betting information is common to both Seven Card Stud and Texas Hold-Em, I will mention it only once in this section and point out any specific differences that apply to Texas Hold-Em in that section.

The only bets players can make before any cards are dealt are either the ante bet, if required by Poker rules at the table you are at, or a so-called "blind bet." A blind bet is a wager you can make before receiving your first cards, or before looking at the cards you have been dealt, and is often used as a ploy by some players, generally those who wish to bluff, or by players who wish to arbitrarily raise the stakes for that game before it begins. It is unlikely that you will encounter players making blind bets in Seven Card Stud, although you will see this quite often in Texas Hold-Em. I recommend you avoid making blind bets, because they can wind up costing you a good deal of money unless you are so savvy in Poker that you can maximize on such a bet with great play and gutsy bluffing when necessary.

"Bluffing" is a key concept in any Poker game, and to bluff means to vigorously overplay a hand of inferior value. Although it is a very good ploy used to great advantage by good Poker players, it can quickly become counterproductive if you're spotted as a bluffer and wind up losing the hand in which you were bluffing. If you intend to bluff at all, the best time to do this is right after you have won big, or won several hands in a row. Chances are that other players will be a little wary of you at that time, thinking that perhaps you in fact do have another great hand, and this is precisely the point of bluffing.

Bluffing is easier in Seven Card Stud than in Texas Hold-Em. In Seven Card Stud your up cards may be showing such a strong hand that other players simply won't risk staying in with you, especially if you are betting as if you really have that hand. If you do in fact have such a great winning hand, it will only reinforce that fear, and thereafter other players will be less likely to call your bluff. And, if you don't overdo it, you can bluff more often and win more often because of this strategy. If, however, you get called on the bluff and lose, don't try it again until you reestablish the strength of your hands and your betting skills. Once you are seen as a bluffer, other players, especially other smart players, will bet into you and you can quickly lose any winnings you have made up to that point.

When any Poker game is in progress, each progression of bets is called a "round." There is one round of betting for each card dealt until all seven cards have been dealt. In each round of betting every player still in the game will be asked to "check," "call," "raise," or "fold."

To check means you wish to stay in the hand without making a bet. It can be done only if no other player before you in turn has made a bet. If the player after you in turn or any other player behind you in position subsequently makes a bet, you must then either call, raise, or fold.

To call means to make the same bet as another player ahead of you in turn, if you wish to make that same bet and not raise it. This also applies if you first check and subsequently another player behind you in turn makes a bet—including any raises made by other players still in the game thereafter—before it again becomes your turn to make that betting decision. To call a bet, you place the same amount of money as bet by that previous player, or players, in front of you and say, "Call." It means you are staying in the round of betting and have bought in for the next round of cards. But don't throw your chips in the pot. This will confuse the dealer, since your chips will scatter around the chips already in the pot and how much you bet will not be clearly seen.

Sometimes the term "see" is used in place of "call." It means the same thing, but is used almost exclusively at the end of the final round of betting, after all cards have been dealt, and only when you are the final person in the hand and you wish to challenge your opponents and see what they have. This is the final bet, and will cost you whatever amount of money has been previously bet by the player, or players, whom you so wish to challenge. This final round of betting is also called the "showdown."

To raise means to increase the amount of the bets made by the players ahead of you in turn. Raises are always allowed only in equal increments of the table's minimum bet requirement, up to the maximum; but quite often the minimum table bet requirement can be used in a raise only in the first and second rounds, and thereafter the higher table bet requirement is the gauge for raise increments.

If you raise, you must say the word "raise" prior to placing your chips in front of you for this bet; if you do not, but simply throw out the chips, chances are that the dealer, and other players for that matter, will assume you are calling the bet only and will not accept the raise. Failing to announce your raise is a severe breach of protocol and often can anger other players whose strategy depends on clear indications from other players on what amounts they bet. This can also, in some instances, annul the game. If you are guilty of this infraction, no amount of pleading will alter the fact that you failed to follow the rules. Other players at the table can, in fact, accuse you of trying to make a "string bet" and demand that the hand be voided. A "string bet" means you don't call a raise and don't announce your intention but are trying to "string" extra money in the pot in order to see how the other players react. Because raising alters betting decisions for all other players, it is important that you clearly announce your decision to raise and then raise by the correct amount.

You can, for example, call a $3 bet while at the same time saying, "Raise three dollars," and place a total of $6 in front of you. This is a clear indication to everyone on the table that you raised the bet.

An important aspect of betting in Poker is a betting ploy called "check and raise." This is allowed in almost all major casino poker rooms and means you check during any round of betting and, if a bet is made by another player and the turn comes back to you before the next card is dealt, you can then raise that bet instead of just calling it, even though you checked initially. This ploy is exploited by smart players to raise the stakes of the pot, especially in circumstances where such a player has a good hand. Check-and-raise options are good for strategy, and can often build up a mediocre pot into a big one.

Still another aspect of betting is folding your hand. To fold means to throw your cards in and get out of that hand. This is a betting decision like all others, and can be used to your advantage if you have a bad hand to start with, or if you don't want to risk your money on a hand with few possibilities. You can fold your hand at any time during the game but only when it's your turn and not before.

Doing this will exclude you from the current hand. You will not receive any more cards and cannot participate in any further action on that hand, and whatever money you had bet up till that point is automatically lost. But by making this no-bet decision you can often save yourself a lot of money that you otherwise would have bet in all the subsequent rounds of betting and could have lost by continuing to play an inferior hand with little win potential. You will get to play again in the next round, and probably receive better cards to play with.

Another method of play—one likely to be employed by bad poker players—is "fishing." Going fishing means having a mediocre hand with some win potential and continuing to bet and play it in the hope that the final card dealt will make that hand into a winner. Players who do this are often called "fishermen," and if they succeed in catching the winning card, such a card is often referred to as having been "caught on the river." It is highly inadvisable to play this way, mostly because of the costs such play will incur in all the rounds of betting up until the final card is dealt, at which point the fisherman finds out if he has caught one or not. If he has, chances are that the fisherman will find himself with the winning hand. It is, however, a far greater likelihood that such a card will not be dealt to him, and the consequences are not just losing money but gaining an immediate reputation as a fisherman at that table.

Once you have been identified as a fisherman, your chances of bluffing become zero and your chances of outplaying your opponents even with good hands will become considerably more difficult than they ordinarily would have been. The up side of fishing is the luck element; but in any Poker game, luck alone—without skill—will make you a winner at best only 10 percent of the time, which plainly means you are likely to lose 90 percent of the hands you are in.

After the dealer shuffles the deck and deals the initial set of cards to each player in the game, the player whose first up card is the lowest in face value of all cards showing has to open the first round of betting (this applies to Seven Card Stud but not Texas Hold-Em, to be discussed shortly). The dealer will almost always point out which player has the lowest card, so don't worry about it if you're unsure.

Whoever has the lowest card must open the game with a bet. After that there are four more rounds of betting to come. At the conclusion of all betting on the first round, the dealer will burn a card, and then deal one card face up to all players still in the game. More betting takes place, and the process is repeated until the last round. If all players but one drop out before the last round, the player still in the game is an automatic winner. In most cases, however, at least two players will stay in the game until the last, the seventh, round—the showdown. It is at this point that the ultimate winner will be decided.

It is also important to remember that should you run out of gaming chips (cash doesn't play) and the hand is still in progress, you are called "all in." If there are more rounds of betting to take place, a side pot will be made for those players who continue the action past your turn. The size of this side pot will depend on the action the table gets after you have been declared all in. You can usually declare this yourself when it's your turn to bet, but to do it you must bet whatever remaining money you have, even though this amount would not normally be enough to continue. You will then still be in the game, but only in the initial pot, and not the side pot. The side pot winners are decided and paid first after the conclusion of all action on that hand. Then the main pot is decided second, and your hand figures in this action. If your hand is the best, you still win the main pot.

Still more important is never to "bet out of turn," that is, make a bet *before* your turn to bet comes. This happens often if players don't pay attention, or are tired and lose track of their turn. This is bad for the person who does it and bad for the other players—particularly so for players still in front of the offender in the turn of bets. A bet out of turn indicates anxiety or carelessness on the part of the culprit.

It tells the other players the state of mind of the offender; these players often alter their betting strategy as a result and use this information to great effect against such an offending player. Sometimes, although not that often, an out-of-turn bet can even annul the game. Do yourself a big favor: If you're too tired, don't play. If you do play, pay sufficient attention not to make silly mistakes like this, which will surely cost you money both in the short term and long run.

In most casinos betting limits for Seven Card Stud begin with $1 to $4 as the lowest limits available, no ante. This means that on any round of betting you can bet as low as $1, or as much as $4, but no less and no more. You can also raise by the same range of amounts, depending on which round of betting it is. Often the pot grows when there are several raises. If one player raises $2, for example, and your turn comes next and you want to raise, you can call the $2 and raise $4, for a total of $6. That's how even small limit games like the so-called 1-to-4 can produce some very decent pots. There is also a game called "1-4-8 on the end." This is the same 1-to-4 game just described, with the added option of betting up to $8 in the final round, after the seventh card has been dealt.

At this point all players still in the game know what their final hands are and, presumably, have what they consider good hands. It is therefore an advantage for players to have the option of betting larger amounts, especially when they think, or know, that they have the winning hand.

Seven Card Stud games offer a variety of betting limits, from the 1-to-4 and the 8-on-the-end option, to the 5-10, 10-20, 20-30 and 50-100. Other higher betting limit games are also available, but very rarely will such a game actually take place in the main casino Poker room. Such high-stakes games are usually played in the private rooms provided by casinos for their high-rolling clientele.

◆| SIMPLE STRATEGY |◆

Your success in Seven Card Stud, and in Poker generally, directly depends on your skill level. Your knowledge of the game and of betting strategies, and your powers of observation regarding other players are all necessary ingredients for winning. Yes, luck of the draw also plays an essential part, but how you conduct your betting for each round and how well you know the cards and the possible winning combinations for *your* set of cards are considerably more important.

Because Seven Card Stud offers you the opportunity of seeing the seven cards you have plus four of the seven cards each of your opponents has—all those players who have stayed with you at least till the sixth card—it is not too difficult to adequately calculate which cards are still left and, to some degree, make adequate judgments on what the likelihood is that your hand will improve with each successive round, all the way to the final, seventh, card. But you don't get to see all the cards. If the table is full, seven players total, not all players will stay in the game. Most will stay to see the fourth card out. Fewer will stay for the fifth card, even fewer for the sixth card.

Because of such player attrition, you will never see all the cards dealt face up, or those that would have been dealt face up had all players stayed in the game. Furthermore, since the dealer always burns a card between rounds, this is another card you don't see. (Burning a card between rounds is done to avoid sequential dealing or the possibility of cheating.) Therefore, depending on the cards you *do* get to see, it is quite important that you make relative judgments as to which of the cards that are left may possibly improve your hand and what the likelihood of getting such a card may be.

On the average, in Seven Card Stud you will see slightly fewer than half the cards in the 52-card deck—sometimes more, and often fewer, depending on the number of players at the table and the number of such players who stay in the hand till the sixth round, also known as "sixth street." Nonetheless, even basic observation will allow you to make some informed choices.

Of those who stayed till sixth street, chances are that most will stay in to see the final card. These are players who already have good hands, or can improve on a good hand, or can have a great hand with just one more card. Of course, there is always the possibility that a player will stay in the hand till the end, bet aggressively, and be bluffing. On occasion you can spot such a bluff, and if you do you can usually outbluff the bluffer. And there can also be people who are the fishermen, players with mediocre hands hoping their one last card will make them winners; these players will mostly stay in each hand by calling the bets, rarely raise, and only begin to bet aggressively if they catch their winning card in the last round.

Whether the remaining players on sixth street will stay in the hand for the final card also depends on the round of betting. If there are four players left, and two bet aggressively, chances are that at least one of the other two will drop out of the hand, not wishing to spend more money for a fishing trip.

But such aggressive players may also be bluffing, so it is important for you to gauge the game and vary your bets. If, for example, you have two pairs—after the sixth round and going into the seventh and final round—and you need one more of either card to make a full house, your chances of drawing such a card depend directly on which cards have already been dealt out. In this example, if you are holding, say, two kings and two jacks, you need either one more king or one more jack to make the full house.

If you've been observant, you may have noticed that

throughout the six rounds two kings have been dealt out. This means all four kings are out. You're holding two, and you saw the other two dealt out. Therefore there is no chance that you can get another king. So you are now reduced to fishing for the jack. But what if you also saw another jack dealt out? That means there is only one card left in the deck that can improve your hand. Of course, you may not have seen these cards dealt out. Another player still in the game may have also been dealt a pair of kings among his initial two down cards (a so-called "pocket pair"), and another player may have a pocket pair of jacks. In either case, how you proceed with your game depends on what you consider the value of your two pairs to be.

Kings and jacks is not a bad hand. If, in evaluating the possible hands other players in the game may have you think that such two high pairs are enough, stay in until the final round. Chances are that you will win with the high two pairs, or may get that extra card for the even better hand. But you should be playing the cards you have and not the cards you *hope* to have, always aware that, in the final tally, your strategy is to play your opponents' hands to lose, not yours to win. But you still have to make certain judgments as to what the possible value of your opponent's hand, or hands if there are more than one player still in the game with you, are. You don't want to get caught playing your own hand badly.

If, to continue our example, you have that high two-pairs hand, and you see another player with four-to-a-flush, chances are that he does have the flush. Therefore your *only* chance of winning is to draw to your full house. If you do, you have a live one and can bet aggressively and likely win a lot from the player with the flush. But if you have seen all but one of the cards that could make you a full house already out, fold. It hurts to fold such a high two-pairs hand, especially if, after the hand is over, you see that the other player really didn't have the flush but only a small pair. This player won because you folded your hand; but because the odds were against your making the full house, folding like this was still smart play no matter what the outcome.

You didn't take a crazy chance, you observed the cards and the play, and you played and bet accordingly. You may have lost this particular hand, but you saved the amount of money that the next bet, and likely series of raises, would certainly have cost you. Over a session in any Poker game this smart play will give you many more winning hands than losing ones.

Also, luck of the draw can be your best friend or your bitter enemy. If you're on the receiving end of a favorable flow of cards, it seems like you can do no wrong. But even if this happens, don't be surprised if you don't win much. It's quite likely that other players at the table will spot the good hands you are getting early in the rounds, and simply not stay in with you. How you bet in these cases will either make you a big winner, or a small winner.

The dilemma is, if you bet aggressively early, you may get other players out and win only little. But if you bet conservatively, not showing the strength of your hand by the bets you make, you could let someone in. This means that a player with a mediocre hand, who probably would have folded had you bet aggressively, will stay in for the hell of it and wind up drawing a better hand than yours. To resolve this dilemma, my simple advice is: *No win is a small win.*

Anytime you are a winner you have made money. If you're not positive you can beat any fisherman, bet to get them out of the game. This is especially important if you've had a run of the cards, won several hands, or won a big pot, and the other players are now scared of you. Now is the time for you to bluff. In this case all you need for a successful bluff is to be showing at least a halfway decent hand. It is almost a given that after such a streak other players will not risk money on even good hands against you, thinking that you again have a great hand.

The second simple advice I can offer you is: *Don't overdo it.* If you bet big consistently, and win big consistently, other players at the table will either leave or simply not stay in the hands you are in until cards turn against you or you make a silly mistake. Making any kind of consistent bets is the telltale sign of a novice player. Always vary your bets—when you bet, how much you bet, as well as how much you raise and when. This way other players will not be able to tell what you have, or anticipate how you will play any given hand.

Also *watch your habits*. Many players display particular behavioral tendencies when holding either good hands, bad hands, or mediocre hands. Players who play Poker regularly will quickly be able to tell what you have even before you realize it.

These signs can be as simple as playing with your gaming chips when you feel good because you see you have a good hand, or scratching your nose when you know you have a bad hand. As with betting, if you must do such small things, be aware of what you're doing and when, and then try to vary or reverse such behavior. This can work in your favor, because these other players watching you will now think you have something other than what you do in fact have.

The third item of simple advice I can offer you is: *Don't be afraid to bet*. Often people new to the game, or new to the casino environment of the game, can underplay their hands. Underplaying good hands, or even marginal hands with good potential, will only result in some other player's drawing a better hand. And this player might not have stayed in the hand with you if you had bet more appropriately to your hand's value. If you are not certain about the quality of your hand, chances are the first impression you got was correct and the hand isn't worth playing. Fold it and play another hand. Only staying in the hand will cost you money, and even if there is an ante at your Seven Card Stud game, losing the half-dollar or dollar ante is better than playing a hand that can result in a greater loss.

At the same time if you do decide to stay in the hand, bet it for all it's worth. Remember the loss limit I mentioned earlier in this book? The same applies here. If you sit at your table with $100, consider that money gone. This is your stake; this is your loss limit. It no longer exists for you. It has become a tool. So use that tool and make it work. Betting safe in Poker is a prescription for disaster. Scared money will fly away quickly, scared to make more. If you see you have a tendency to play this way, take a break, or leave and play later. This also applies if you are not getting any decent cards with which to play. However, betting safe is different from betting conservatively. Betting safe means you underplay a good hand. Betting conservatively means you don't overplay a marginal hand and never play a bad hand.

As my final piece of advice for Seven Card Stud, and Poker in general, I reiterate: *Don't play your hand as a potential winner—play your opponents' hands as potential losers.* This may sound like a contradiction in attitude, but it does have certain value. If you play your cards as a potential winner, and there are three other people still in the game with you, odds are 3:1 against you that one of these other three players has a hand better than yours.

If you always play your hand as a potential winner, you're playing Poker like an ostrich. You stick your head in the sand and hope the danger will go away. In all gambling games, but Poker especially, until the hand is over and the winner is decided, there's always a possibility that what you think of as a winning hand will wind up second best, or worse, third best. Time and time again I have seen players feel ever so confident in their hand, yet lose in the final round because they played their hand to win, rather than their opponent's hand to lose.

Again this comes down to your Poker acumen, knowledge of the game, your betting strategy, and how well you keep track of your opponents' possible hands. Playing your opponents' hands to lose rather than your hand to win means that you shift the focus of your attention from feeling comfortable about your hand's possibilities to anticipating the possible failures in your opponents' hands.

If you have a good hand in Poker and have possibilities to improve it still, you already know what you have and what you need to make it better, as discussed in the examples above. Therefore, your hand should command little or no attention from now on. Your hand and its possibilities for improvement are a fact you have already calculated and are aware of, while your opponents are not.

At this point you should focus on those players who are still in the game with you and take a quick calculation of what their apparent hands, and likely improvements, may be. These decisions come into play in Seven Card Stud mostly in the fifth round, so-called "fifth street" and again on sixth street. But the crucial point is the fifth card out. By this time it is already possible for any player still in the game to possess a great hand. After all, only five of the seven cards can be used to make a winning hand. And because Seven Card Stud offers you the chance of seeing three of the first five cards, fairly accurate judgments of hand potential are possible, if you look and pay attention to what you are seeing.

While other players are busy making judgments of what hand *you* may possibly have, you already know. Therefore, devote your energy and powers of observation to what your opponents have, or can make out of what they have. This constitutes smart play in Poker, because your hand is only as good as your opponent's hand is bad. You may hold four aces, but if your opponent draws a straight flush, your hand isn't worth a plugged nickel. In this example, if you played your four aces to the hilt and didn't bother to see the straight flush draw one of your opponents had, you'd be broke in one hand. Therefore don't play your hand to win, but play your opponent's hand to lose.

◆| TEXAS HOLD-EM |◆

Texas Hold-Em resembles Seven Card Stud only in that a total of seven cards are dealt out in the end, and that five of the seven cards are used by players to make the best possible hand they can. But this is where the similarity ends.

In Texas Hold-Em—generally known simply as "Hold-Em"—all players at the table get two cards face down, which only they can see, but the remaining five cards are dealt out face up, in front of the dealer, and are *common* cards to *all* the players in the game. This means that if these five common cards have among them, say, two kings, those two kings are common to *everyone* at the table who is still in the game at that point. All players can use these kings to combine with the two cards they have, plus any of the remaining cards among the common cards.

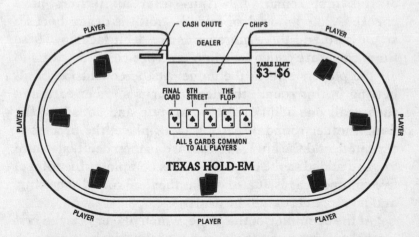

A game of Texas Hold-Em in progress. Note the two cards dealt face down to each player and the five other cards shared in common.

♦| HOW THE GAME IS PLAYED |♦

Texas Hold-Em tables are usually bigger than Seven Card Stud tables, and generally accommodate from seven to twelve players. In some casinos games accommodating up to fourteen players are also offered. As in all Poker games, dealing begins after the dealer shuffles the cards. The game uses the standard 52-card deck, with no jokers and no wild cards. Following the shuffle, the dealer will burn from three to five cards, depending on House rules. He then begins to deal clockwise. Each player at the Hold-Em table is given a total of two down cards—dealt one by one in turn—but only after two of the players have made their mandatory ante bets (I will discuss this shortly in greater detail).

After these two down cards are dealt to each player, the first round of betting takes place. It is only at the conclusion of this first round of betting—after all players have checked, called, raised, or folded—that the dealer burns a single card and three more cards are dealt face up. These three cards are called "the flop" and are common cards to all the players still in the game. At the conclusion of all betting in this round, the dealer burns another card and then deals one additional card face up and adds it to the flop. Another round of betting takes place, the process is repeated, and the final seventh card is then dealt, also face up, and added to the other four. This completes the total of five common cards. It also begins the final round of betting, and no more cards will be dealt.

At the beginning of the game, which player gets the first card out depends on the position of the "dealer's puck," a small, round, white plastic object similar to that used in Craps, except that in Hold-Em it has two white sides each of which has the word "dealer" written on it. The puck moves from player to player clockwise after each deal, so that no single player will always get the first card out, and to prevent any one player from always having to be the first one to make a bet. This is also done to make sure that all players at the table will eventually have to put up their mandatory ante bets (again, more on this a little further on).

Whoever holds the puck will get the last card dealt at each turn of the deal. The player sitting to the left of the player with the dealer's puck gets the first card, the player to his left the next card, and so on. The player to the left of the player holding the puck also has to make an ante bet in an amount equal to the table minimum, and the player next to him, on his left, has to make a second ante bet equal to one-third of that amount, both mandatory bets in Hold-Em. Technically, these first bets are really blind bets—that is, bets on your own cards before you've seen them—rather than ante bets, but they are nonetheless called an ante.

These ante amounts vary depending on the table limits. Since the puck moves from player to player around the table after each hand is completed, eventually all players will have to make such blind bets. This double-ante requirement is there for three basic reasons: first, because players making such bets are in the favored spot, getting the first and second card out respectively; second, because the player with the higher ante bet is now able to see how all the other players play and bet before having to make any further decisions; and third, to place some action on the table. If there is no action, and all players fold except one player, that player still gets a small win. In addition, the player who had to make the bigger ante bet also gets a chance to raise the bets at the end of the first round of betting. This opportunity to so raise the bets is called an "option."

If you do not make the ante bet when it is your turn, or call yourself out of that hand, or if you were not present at the table when it was your turn to put up the ante, you get no cards and now have to wait until the puck comes back around to you in order to be allowed to play again. You can, however, buy yourself back in the game at any time after you missed your blind bet turn, by betting *both* ante bets out of turn.

The player making the smaller ante bet will be the first player asked to bet or fold after both initial cards are dealt to all players, since the player making the higher ante bet is considered to already have made the minimum required bet. The first round of betting now takes place among the remaining players. When all players have checked, bet, raised and/or called and/or folded, the flop takes place, and thereafter the remaining rounds of betting, as indicated earlier.

At the final round, when all the remaining active players have called all the bets, the showdown takes place. These players turn over their two hole cards—that is, the two down cards that make up their individual hands—and the dealer will make the best comparison between each player's set of two hole cards and the five common cards. Whichever player has the best five-card Poker hand, using his two hole cards and any of the five common cards, is declared the winner and gets the pot.

♦| HOW TO BET |♦

Many Hold-Em games start with the $1-to-$3 limit, but the majority of games are usually of the $3-to-$6 variety. Other games offer the "3-6-12 on the end" option, meaning that in the last round players can bet up to $12 and raise up to $12. Still other games offer 5-to-10, 25-to-50 and even 100-to-200 limits, but generally the game you are likely to encounter most often is the 3-to-6 limit game. I will, therefore, outline the sequence of bets using the 3-to-6 game as basis for the examples.

Let's say that you are *not* one of the players required to make the $3 or $1 ante blind bet at the beginning of the new deal. In this case you get the first two cards without having to make any bets—yet. After you get the first two cards, face down so only you can see them, the first round of betting occurs.

If you think your two-card hand is good enough for you to take a chance on playing at least to the flop, which most players will do, you wait your turn and then bet accordingly. Each player, at each round of betting, can check, call, raise and check-and-raise, or fold. The only exception is in the first round of betting, because the two ante bets are already in action; therefore no player can check, but must either call, raise, or fold.

If you *are* one of these players next to the dealer's puck, you have already bet $3 or $1, depending on whether you are the first or second player in turn, and therefore you *cannot* check on the opening round. Your *only* option is to call, raise, or fold. If, however, you are the player who is required to make the $3 blind bet and your first two down cards are so bad that you would normally have folded the hand if they were dealt to you at a different position in the betting turn, don't automatically fold if all players just call this first-action bet. If that should happen, and you do have a bad hand, throwing it away makes no sense since you have already bought your way into the flop round. Who knows? The flop may turn your bad hand into the winning hand. I've seen that happen often enough. If, however, players at the table raise the bets, and it comes back to you and your hand looks like trash, fold and get out.

But if you have a good hand, and you are that player who made the $3 blind bet, and all other players simply call this action, you can now exercise your option to raise the bets. Then all the other players at the table have to call, raise, or fold, and it goes around again until all players make their decisions. Only then will the next round begin. In almost all casino Poker games there's a limit of three raises per round if more than two players are in the game. If there are only two players left betting, they can raise each other until doomsday, or until one of them is "all in," meaning he has no more active gaming chips on the table with which to bet. Eventually either this happens or one of the players calls the other and we're back at the showdown—the best Poker hand wins.

◆| SIMPLE STRATEGY |◆

As I've said before, apart from the hierarchy of hands, there are practically no rules in Texas Hold-Em that can be listed as "always must do" or "never do." By its very nature, Poker is a game of almost infinite variety; for any strategy play, therefore, the best advice I can offer you is a few examples of what may occur in a sample hand, together with a few hints designed to give you a heads-up start. These examples are indications of what can be the best way to play such hands; of course when you actually play Hold-Em, chances are you will get very different hands.

To list every possible hand in Hold-Em would require an encyclopedia, and we haven't the space to create one here—nor, I imagine, would you want to read one. But the examples I have chosen will give you an indication of the kind of strategy play that will make your Hold-Em play smarter. Yes, you will need to adapt what I am suggesting to the nearly infinite variety of Hold-Em hands you are likely to encounter in an actual game, but my purpose here is to provide a framework that will give you indications of how you can best apply the strategy suggestions I have made in this chapter on Poker, and in this book in general.

Let's say that you are one of the players at a Texas Hold-Em table, and you have an ace of clubs and a jack of diamonds as your two down cards, which only you can see. On the flop you may see this:

Ace of Diamonds—6 of Diamonds—3 of Clubs

Therefore, so far you have: two aces and three-to-the-diamond flush. Let's say that the next card out is the jack of clubs. You now have two pairs: two aces and two jacks. But you also have three to the flush in both diamonds and clubs. Since there is only one more card to be dealt, whatever that card is you cannot make a flush in either clubs or diamonds. Therefore the hand you are playing is the two pairs—the two aces and the two jacks—with the possible draw of either a jack or an ace on the final card to make you a full house.

At this point you should once again remember that all the common cards can be used by all the other players still in the hand with you. And, unlike in Seven Card Stud, although you see these exposed cards, you cannot make the same kind of judgments on the possible values of your opponents' hands. One of your opponents may have two clubs in hand, or two diamonds, and therefore need only either one to make a flush.

In this case if you don't get the full house your two pairs will be no good against such a flush, if indeed that player does draw to make it. Therefore, in such a case, in order to determine what you should do next, you should estimate how many diamonds and clubs have already been dealt out.

There are thirteen of each suit in a 52-card deck; between your two down cards and the flop you see three of each of the two suits that matter to you, and to your opponent, who you think may be holding two cards suited to the flush draw. This means that there are ten possible cards still unknown to you that can make that other player a flush. Depending on the number of players at your table, a fair guess would be that at least five of each of the suits that matter to you have already been dealt out, or are among the burn cards; on this basis you can then assume that the other player's chances are 1 in 5 that the final card in this hand will turn out to be the one suit he needs to make the flush.

Next, you should take into account the value of each suited card exposed. Since you have the ace and the jack, the biggest cards left are the king and the queen. If both are showing among the common cards, then you know that, at best, the other player can have a 10-high flush draw. If only one is showing, then you know the other player could have the other card as his high draw. Once you have decided this, you can then practice the "play the other player's hand to lose" principle I mentioned earlier. If neither the king nor the queen is showing on the board—among the common cards seen so far—you know that the other player can have, at best, both the king and the queen as his high draw-to-the-flush. Chances are that his hand is paired up to at least one pair thus far, so you know that if he doesn't hit the flush, the best hand he can come up with is two pairs, with the high pair being either the kings or the queens. But since you already have two pairs one of which is the pair of aces, your two pairs are already far superior to any hand the other player may get, other than the flush.

Plus, you still have the last card draw to your full house. When you weigh these options together, it is easy to see that your chances of hitting a full house are equal to the other player's chances of drawing to the flush and that under the worst circumstances, where neither you nor he makes a better hand, your high two pairs are already a winner. So, now it is time for you to raise the bet and reraise if you are raised in turn. Then wait to see what the last card out is. If it is either one of the two suits you think that other player needs to make his flush, just check, if it is your turn, and then see; or, if it's the other player's turn to bet, just call him and see.

In either case your overall chances of beating him are better than his chances of beating you. And, if you do make the full house, keep betting and raising until you are called. You're likely to win a big pot.

It is for reasons like this that betting and playing strategy in Hold-Em is vastly different from Seven Card Stud. Many hands such as I described above will occur regularly in Hold-Em. But another great aspect of the game is that in Hold-Em it is possible to win a pot with absolute garbage in hand. A hand that looks great, potentially, with the first two cards, can turn to garbage on the flop. How you play the hand from then on will determine if you win and how much.

For example, you may have the ace and queen of spades as your two hole cards—not a great beginning hand but a good hand to stay with to the flop—but on the flop the three cards showing may fall as: 2 of clubs, 8 of diamonds, and 10 of hearts. Garbage as far as your hand is concerned. There is nothing you can do with this hand unless you pull an ace or queen in the next two cards, still to come, to make a pair. Maybe even two pairs if you're very lucky. But, practically speaking, this hand is trash. However, you have a high hand, relative to the flop.

If, for the sake of this example, no other cards come out that make any pair or any hand for any player at the table, your ace-queen combination is quite likely to be the winner. In essence, your garbage is better than someone else's garbage. The only hand that can beat you is an ace-king combination. In this example, you should be able to tell if another player has a better hand than you by the way he bets. Of course he, or the other players who also bet like this, may be trying to "buy" the pot, meaning they have nothing but bet aggressively, trying to give the other players the impression they have something—a more vigorous version of bluffing—well aware that the flop shows garbage. Most of the time this ploy works if indeed all the other players also have bad hands and simply decide it's not worth the risk of spending more money on the off chance the aggressive bettor is actually bluffing.

Also, in some circumstances, if, say, you and another player hammer this out to the end, and both of you have an ace-queen, the hand will be a tie and the pot split between you. Sometimes, however, there may be an open pair on board, meaning that the winning hand is common to all players. This is called "playing the board," meaning that your two hole cards may not figure in the best possible Poker hand combination, depending on what unpaired hole cards you and the other players hold.

If this happens, and you have the ace-queen and your one other opponent has, say, queen-jack, your ace will play and you win. The hierarchy of Poker hands applies, and the best possible hand wins even if this winning hand simply constitutes that lone ace. A hand with such a lone winning ace is often called "ace in the hole."

Another hint that I can offer you applies to the first round of betting. If you are the player who had to make the bigger ante bet, exercise your option to raise when all other players simply call. This will allow you to quickly determine which players have the stronger hands. Usually some players will fold, and most will call. If, however, another player raises again, you now have to determine whether that player has a good hand and played the check-and-raise strategy or is bluffing and wants to see how strong your hand is. How you play this hand from now on depends entirely on your skill level, what confidence you have in yourself and your cards, and on what your betting relationship has been thus far with the other players on previous hands. In most instances it is best to raise the bet again, in which case it is quite likely that the battle for the pot will take place mostly between you and the player who challenged you. Or, you may simply call the bet and see how the other player bets following the flop. In this way you will not showcase the strength of your hand and will, in effect, challenge the other player to make the next move first. But in this circumstance, as in all others, the possibilities are so many that each event has to be treated independently and acted on as it occurs. There are no rules that can be offered which will tell you always to do this or always do that. In Poker, and Hold-Em especially, whether you win or lose depends less on what cards you have or will draw than on how you play each hand and each round of betting. It is for this reason that almost all of my suggestions on Poker strategy are by examples. There simply are no hard-and-fast rules to list.

I will therefore offer the following few hints as introduction to simple strategy for Texas Hold-Em:

1. Stay in the opening round to see the flop if you have at least an ace-king, off suit, or at least king-queen, suited.

2. If you stay in the opening round, before the flop, call the bets made by other players and raise only if other players have bet or called without hesitation. Remember that you cannot check on the opening round in Hold-Em, because the ante bets are already in action as blind bets. If other players raise these bets more than once, and you have no pocket pair and no ace in the hole, fold if you don't improve your hand on the flop.

3. If you have a pocket pair, call if it's a low pair (deuces through tens); raise if you have a pocket pair of jacks or queens; raise and reraise, if possible, if you have a pocket pair of kings or aces.

4. After the flop, if your hand improves marginally but it is not your turn to open the betting, wait to find out how the other players bet before you decide what to do. If they bet aggressively, and several raises take place before it is your turn, call the bets. If one player bets but no other players raise, then you raise. If you are reraised, call. If it's your turn to open the betting, check and see what happens. If there are bets from other players but no raises, check-and-

raise. If you are raised, call. If you have a *great* hand after the flop, say three of a kind, two high pairs, or even better, bet the maximum allowed for that round and see what happens. Chances are you will be called. If you are raised, call, and don't reraise. At this point, with a great hand, you don't want to overplay the hand and get other players to drop out before you can get more of their money into the pot.

5. Fold your hand on sixth street only if it is merely marginal, is not improved by the sixth card dealt, and if the other players bet too big relative to your pot investment so far. Always fold your hand anytime you're not sure it can win, especially if other players at the table bet vigorously. Chances are your hunch is right and you would merely have fed the pot.

6. On sixth street, if your hand does improve, bet it to the hilt. Now is the time to get other players out of the game. If other players are fishing, your hard action will tell them to watch out, and chances are they will fold and thus not place you in danger of losing your good hand by getting lucky on the last card. However, if some other player bets into *you* aggressively, chances are that player also has a good hand, maybe a better hand than you. In that case raise him two times, and if he raises again, call him. If you do not improve your hand, but still have the good hand you started with, check and call if it's your turn first, or raise once and then call if you are reraised. If you are not reraised, it tells you that the other player still needs to improve his hand, or is not sure of how good your hand is. This will set up your strategy for the last round.

7. When the final, seventh, card is dealt, and it's your turn to open the betting, bet as aggressively as in

sixth street, *regardless* of what the last card meant to your hand. If it's not your turn to open the betting, wait to see what other players do. If other players still in the game bet aggressively—especially that one player who has consistently challenged you— and he or one of the other players still in the game raises before it comes to your turn, reraise the bets again, but only call when the betting comes back to you if your reraised bet is raised yet again. If other players in front of you in turn simply bet and call, and your turn comes, raise. If called, chances are you have the winning hand. If raised again, call, but look at the flop and see what possibilities there may be for such a player before you make the final call bet. If you need time to think, you can call "time." Calling time is to your advantage only in this case, because the other players will wonder whether you are think- ing of raising again. In fact, what you are doing is taking a final look at the board to clarify your calcu- lations, but you have already decided to call. But asking for time in any other circumstance will work to your disadvantage because it shows uncertainty on your part and is a sign of weakness and care- lessness.

If you're pretty sure you still have the winning hand, calling this bet under the circumstances I de- scribed is better than raising again only to find out the other player did pick up a winner on the last card. At this point the amount of your call bet is small relative to the amount you have already in- vested in the pot, so such a call is worth the risk even if you are marginally unsure of the other player's hand. But raising the bet in this circumstance could result in your being caught in the war of raises, and, should that other player actually beat you, cost you too much money relative to your pot investment up to that point.

8. Don't bluff. Unlike in Seven Card Stud, bluffing in Hold-Em can cost you a lot. There are simply too many possibilities that can allow other players to make better hands than the one you've got if you try to bluff. I've seen players bluff only to be called on the bluff by a good player and beat with a lowly pair of deuces or even just ace high.

9. Just as important as not overplaying your good hand is not underplaying a bad hand. A bad hand may look marginal at the opening round, maybe even after the flop, yet quickly turn good on sixth street.

    Sometimes, especially in the opening round before the flop, if the action is heavy, you can build yourself a pot by overplaying a hand that normally you wouldn't bet so big. Usually, if this happens, other players at the table also have marginal hands and you can get yourself a winner by making them all think you're the power at the table. But don't do it too often, because this is a borderline bluff. If you're lucky on the draw, you may wind up looking as good as you were betting, but if you're not so lucky, you can easily get called and caught. Once you are caught bluffing, or overplaying a marginal hand, your odds of winning on sloppy hands goes down the drain. In both the short term and long run, you're better off playing it straight.

I'm certain that by now you get the idea of how complex casino Poker is. Playing Poker at home with friends allows for flexibility that casino Poker simply does not have. In casino Poker, chances are that at least one of the people at your table will be a professional. Sometimes there are two pros at the table, playing in teams. If you approach casino Poker with the home-town-poker-player attitude you'll get cleaned out quickly. Casino Poker is a great game to enjoy, but be wary of what you're getting into. Poker is a game of many skills. Relying on pure luck will surely make you a loser.

But to play smart requires at least a grasp of the basics, knowing what your choices are, when to apply them, and why you are making them. This approach will provide you with a rewarding Poker experience, and with the knowledge that you can hold your own playing Poker in the casino environment.

One final piece of small advice: Don't get distracted by this casino environment—the noise, hustle, cocktail girls, talk at the table, or antics by some players. Play your cards, be cool, don't drink, and watch other players and how they play. This too will help make you a smart Poker player.

9
BIG BOARD KENO

♥ ◆ ♣ ♠

What I call Big Board Keno is mostly known in casinos simply as Keno, but with the advent of Video Keno, I think it important to differentiate between these two games. I have therefore coined this expression as a means of identifying that particular Keno game played in the Keno lounge, with cash money instead of coins and displayed throughout the casino on big illuminated boards.

Big Board Keno was at one time called the Chinese Lottery. This is because the game originated in ancient China. What we now know as lotteries all evolved from this Chinese game. We can therefore thank Marco Polo both for introducing us to spaghetti and for bringing Keno from behind the Great Wall of China and into western culture. Throughout the centuries this game has remained virtually unaltered. This is perhaps because the way it is played is so simple that no alterations to its basic principles were ever needed. The only modifications, especially for modern casino play, lie in the amounts of money you can win, and in the use of combination tickets, called "way tickets."

♦| HOW TO RECOGNIZE BIG BOARD KENO |♦

Almost every major casino offers Big Board Keno. It is easy to recognize because it is played in the Keno lounge, an area usually the size of a large living room, and in some cases larger still. In this lounge are several rows of comfortable chairs for players to sit on, each equipped with a rack containing blank Keno tickets, Keno markers, and booklets on how to play the game. These booklets show the various options of play as offered in this casino, and also list the minimum bet requirements and amounts that the wagers will pay if winning combinations are achieved.

In front of these rows of chairs is the Keno counter, which is the area where bets are taken, tickets written, and payments made to winners. Behind the counter is the work area, where employees run the game. In this work area is a round wire "bird cage," or, in some casinos, a different device that looks like a plastic bubble; this "bubble" is also round and about the size of an inflated beach ball. The main difference between these two devices is in how they are used to draw the Keno numbers.

The wire bird cage rotates to draw the numbers, which are printed on ping pong balls, while the bubble uses forced air to blow the numbers up a tube and into two separate V-shaped arms mounted atop the bubble. To simplify explanations, I shall primarily refer to the wire bird cage as the main device for drawing Keno numbers from now on, unless it becomes necessary to mention the bubble in context.

In the bird cage are 80 Ping-Pong balls, painted with numbers from 1 through 80. When the game is played, this bird cage rotates and spits out 20 of the 80 numbers. These 20 numbers constitute the result of that particular game, and a player picking any combination of them wins.

Mounted over the work area and bird cage is the famous Big Board. This board displays 80 numbers corresponding to the numbers on the Ping-Pong balls in the bird cage. As the numbers are drawn at random, during the calling of the Keno game, each number, as drawn, lights up on the Big Board. This is done so that players can easily see what numbers have been drawn. Such boards are also found throughout the casino, mounted over bars, in other gaming areas, and even in restaurants. This is done partly to publicize the game, but mainly to offer players easy access to results of the game. Players do not have to be in the Keno lounge to play Keno.

Almost all casinos also offer the services of Keno runners, who run tickets for players who wish to play Keno but don't want to sit in the Keno lounge. Keno runners are available to any player in any area of the casino. If you are at the bar or at a gaming table, and you want to also play Keno, just ask for a Keno runner and one will be sent to you. This Keno runner will then return to you for each game played and will continue to come to you until you decide to stop playing. Players eating in the restaurants, for instance, often pass the time by playing Keno this way, using the Keno runners to make their bets and collect their winnings.

The Big Board used to display winning numbers
in Big Board Keno.

◆| HOW TO PLAY BIG BOARD KENO |◆

If you know how to play the state lottery, then you already know the basics of playing casino Big Board Keno. Like the lottery, Big Board Keno involves betting on a single number or set of numbers which you can choose as you wish, in the hope that your number or numbers will be selected in a random drawing. There are, however, substantial differences from the lottery—not so much in the way the game is played, as in the variety of ways you can play it. These options offer much more enjoyment, and often many more wins, than any lottery.

On any Keno game you can pick from one to twenty numbers. You do this by taking a blank Keno ticket and, with the Keno marker provided at any Keno location, simply marking the numbers you wish to play. The Keno ticket is about 5 inches square, and on the face of it is a printed grid of 80 numbers divided into what is called the "top"—containing 40 numbers, and the "bottom"—containing the other 40 numbers. You can mark these numbers by crosses, or circles, ticks, or in any manner, so long as you make it clear that you are marking a specific number. Once you have marked the ticket with the numbers you wish to play, you mark the amount you want to bet in the top right-hand corner of the ticket, where it says "Amount." Then below on the right-hand side, you write the total number of numbers you picked and take the ticket to the Keno writer, who sits behind the Keno counter.

Since most Keno games are now computerized, the Keno writer will generally take your marked ticket, place it over a computer display the size of which corresponds to the size of your Keno ticket, press the numbers you picked, enter the amount you are betting, enter the number of games you wish to play, and then press a button marked "video." The computer will then print out a computerized version of the ticket you marked, which, once you've paid the amount of your bet, the Keno writer gives to you.

This computerized printout corresponds directly to the ticket you had marked, but also includes other information such as game number, ticket code, writer's code, date and time of purchase. This ticket can also include your account number, if you are a regular Keno player and wish your action to be tracked for casino rating purposes; and it can also list the number of consecutive games played if you play your numbers for more than one game. (In the old days tickets were marked by hand, using a messy black ink. This was time-consuming and often resulted in writer error. Since Keno is already a pretty slow game compared to

KENO

ACCOUNT NO.	PRICE PER GAME
NO. OF GAMES	TOTAL PRICE

MARK NUMBER OF SPOTS OR WAYS PLAYED

WINNING TICKETS MUST BE COLLECTED IMMEDIATELY AFTER EACH KENO GAME IS CALLED

1	2	3	4	5	6	7	8	9	10
11	12	13	14	15	16	17	18	19	20
21	22	23	24	25	26	27	28	29	30
31	32	33	34	35	36	37	38	39	40

WE PAY ON COMPUTER ISSUED TICKETS - TICKETS WITH ERRORS NOT CORRECTED BEFORE START OF GAME WILL BE ACCEPTED AS ISSUED

41	42	43	44	45	46	47	48	49	50
51	52	53	54	55	56	57	58	59	60
61	62	63	64	65	66	67	68	69	70
71	72	73	74	75	76	77	78	79	80

WE ARE NOT RESPONISIBLE FOR KENO RUNNERS TICKETS NOT VALIDATED BEFORE START OF NEXT GAME

A Big Board Keno ticket.

other games in the casino, the advantages of computerization are obvious.) It is important that you hold on to your computerized ticket. You will need to produce it in order to collect any winnings to which you are entitled.

In order to claim your winnings, you must also remember to return to the Keno counter at the completion of your game, and *before the start of the next game*. Many players often stray away, distracted, and forget to claim their winning tickets before the next game. But gaming regulations stipulate that winnings must be collected on any ticket prior to the start of the next game. If you fail to do this, you forfeit any winnings.

Keno also allows for so-called "multirace" tickets. With this option you can play whatever numbers you pick on the same ticket for up to 20 consecutive games. You must, however, play the *same* numbers for each game and, of course, the cost of your bet will increase proportionately to the number of games you play. With multirace tickets you cannot claim any winnings at the end of each game, but must wait until the final game in your series has been called. This can be a long wait, especially if you play up to 20 games in a row, which is the maximum number of consecutive races allowed on such tickets. So, to give players the option of doing something else while playing Keno, and to combat complaints from those unlucky lucky players who win but forget to claim their prizes on time, a new multirace variation often called "stray and play" Keno has been introduced at many casinos in Nevada.

This option allows players to play from 21 to 1,000 consecutive games *without having to be present* and with up to one year to collect winnings. You can actually go back home, then mail in your ticket a few weeks later, or even keep it and come back the next year and the winnings are still yours to collect.

♦| STRAIGHT UP |♦

There are four basic betting options offered by most casinos, of which the simplest and most common is the "straight up" ticket, commonly known as the "regular game" ticket. Playing this way is most similar to playing a lottery. It requires merely that you select the numbers you wish to play and choose how much you wish to bet, then mark those numbers straight up, meaning not in any particular combinations. Your winnings depend on how many numbers of those you selected are drawn in the game you are playing, and how much you bet.

For example, a popular straight up ticket is a 6-spot. This means that you select any six of the 80 numbers available in the game. When the game is then played, the bird cage machine draws 20 of the 80 available numbers. If, out of those 20, at least three of the numbers you picked are drawn, you win a small amount—more if four of your numbers are among the 20 drawn in that game, more still if five are drawn, and the jackpot if all six of the numbers you picked are among the 20 out of possible 80 drawn during the calling of that game.

A typical payoff for a $2 bet on a 6-spot Keno ticket would run as follows:

0	out of	6	=	no win	
1	out of	6	=	no win	
2	out of	6	=	no win	
3	out of	6	=	$2	
4	out of	6	=	$6	
5	out of	6	=	$176	
6	out of	6	=	$3,000	the jackpot, and most that can be won on this bet.

You can, of course, also bet more than the required minimum. A bet of $5 will give you a top jackpot win of

$7,500; a bet of $15 pays $22,500; a bet of $30 quite a bit more, and so on. You can bet up to $70 in this way in most casinos.

Although at most of the bigger casinos in Las Vegas and other gaming centers throughout the country, the minimum required bet is generally $2, other casinos offer lower minimums, often as low as forty cents per ticket per game. The common average is $1 per game. Of course your payoffs are lower as well, and in some of these casinos you need to catch at least four out of your six numbers in order to get your money back.

Although the 6-spot bet is among the best and also the most common in straight up Keno betting, all casinos will allow you to select from just a single number up to 10 numbers. Some casinos also offer 12-, 13-, 14-, 15-, and 16-number straight up tickets as well. Of course, the more numbers you pick, the harder it is to win the jackpot, although the payoffs can ultimately be much higher.

• | WAY TICKETS | •

Substantially different from straight up tickets, in which you are effectively betting on single numbers, so called "way" tickets are combination tickets whereby you can pick and bet on several *groups* of numbers. If, for example, you were to play 6 numbers as a way ticket, you could create three groups of two numbers, or two groups of three numbers.

To be more specific, let's say you marked two groups of three numbers each. This you do by placing a circle, or as close to a circle as possible, around the group of three numbers that you want to become your first group of three, and another such circle around the second group of three numbers. You can also play this ticket as one group of four and one group of two, or any other group combination that, together, contains a total of six numbers.

With a ticket like this—if you are playing it as, say, two groups of three numbers—you are betting not only on one group of six numbers, but at the same time on two groups of three numbers. You would therefore, in the appropriate place at the top of the ticket, mark the ticket "⅔," to indicate that you are betting on "two threes," and just below this "⅙," to indicate that you are also betting on "one six." You now have essentially one 6-spot ticket and two 3-spot tickets. In this example, if you hit either of the two groups of three, you would win the amount corresponding to a 3-spot ticket. Furthermore, you still get a payoff on any three, four, five, and six numbers from the 6-spot ticket. Indeed, if all six numbers are drawn, you win *both* the 3-spot bets, *and* the 6-spot.

The main advantage of betting a way ticket is, therefore, that you can play more game options on the same ticket with the same numbers. In addition, winnings are multiplied. The amount of such winnings depends on how many numbers in any way group were hit in combination with any other numbers in one, or more, of your other way groups. For example, if you play the ⅔–⅙ ticket and hit three numbers in one group of three and two numbers in the other group of three, you will be paid 3-for-3 in the one group *plus* 2-in-3 for the other group *plus* 5-in-6 for *both* groups.

Such multiplication of wins is fairly easy to understand in this simple example, but can get very complex on tickets with multiple groups. Don't worry about it, because the computer will calculate all your winnings automatically. All you need to remember is that by playing a way ticket you do not rely on hitting just specific single numbers, but can win—and win a lot—by hitting combinations of your numbers in several of the groups you picked.

Although the minimum bet requirement for a straight up ticket may be $2 per game, in most casinos a way ticket can be played at reduced rates. For example, this ⅔–⅙ ticket can be played at $1 *per way*, for a total cost of $3—

calculated as $1 on each of the two threes, and $1 on the six. Needless to say, your betting options can get very complex. You could, for example, pick a way ticket with the following groups: Three ones (known as "kings"), two groups of two, and five groups of three. Such a ticket will give you the following way-ticket combinations: ³⁄₁, ³⁄₂, ¹²⁄₃, ²²⁄₄, ³⁰⁄₅, ⁴⁸⁄₆, ⁶⁹⁄₇, ⁷⁵⁄₈, ⁹⁵⁄₉ and ¹⁰⁵⁄₁₀—plus several combinations of 11, 12, 13, 14, 15, and 20, for which most casinos do not offer payoffs.

The above combination list simply means that this ticket can produce many winners. For example, it allows you twelve ways to win on a 3-spot (marked above as: ¹²⁄₃) and forty-eight ways to win on a 6-spot (marked above as: ⁴⁸⁄₆).

Such a ticket will, of course, cost you more money to play, if you play *all* the options. You can, however play the ticket just one way, say, the ⁴⁸⁄₆, which will cost you $48 for a $1-per-way price. Actually, casinos frequently offer even further reduced rates for way tickets such as these, as low as a dime per way.

A way ticket like this will allow you to pick 22 total numbers, and multiply your chances of hitting a winning combination. Let's say you play this ticket as a ⁴⁸⁄₆—if any six numbers drawn fit into *any of the groups you marked* on such a way ticket, you will win the 6-spot jackpot. (In addition, if, say, twelve of these numbers within your groups are picked, you then win a multiple of 6-spot jackpots, *as well as* all the smaller pays in between, all multiplied together several times.) This way of playing Keno is not only an excellent way to multiply your jackpots, but I'd recommend it as the only way you should play it.

There are many such way tickets possible, and way ticket combinations are limited only by your imagination and the casino betting limits. The Keno booklets provided by the casinos often list several of the more popular way-ticket options. One such popular ticket, known as "8

KENO

ACCOUNT NO.

PRICE PER GAME
$2.00

MARK NUMBER OF SPOTS OR WAYS PLAYED
1/6

NO. OF GAMES
1

TOTAL PRICE
$2.00

WINNING TICKETS MUST BE COLLECTED IMMEDIATELY AFTER EACH KENO GAME IS CALLED

1	2	3	4	5	6	7	8	9	10
11	12	13	14	15	16	17	18	19	20
21	22	✗	24	25	26	27	28	29	30
31	32	33	34	35	36	37	38	39	40

WE PAY ON COMPUTER ISSUED TICKETS - TICKETS WITH ERRORS NOT CORRECTED BEFORE START OF GAME WILL BE ACCEPTED AS ISSUED

41	42	43	44	✗	✗	47	48	49	50
51	52	53	✗	55	56	57	58	59	60
61	62	✗	✗	6					
71	72	73	74	7					

WE ARE NOT RESPONSIBLE FOR KENO RUNNER

KENO

ACCOUNT NO.

PRICE PER GAME
3.00

MARK NUMBER OF SPOTS OR WAYS PLAYED
2/3   1/6

NO. OF GAMES
1

TOTAL PRICE
$3.00

WINNING TICKETS MUST BE COLLECTED IMMEDIATELY AFTER EACH KENO GAME IS CALLED

1	2	3	4	5	6	7	8	9	10
11	12	13	✗	15	16	17	18	19	20
21	22	23	24	25	✗	27	28	29	30
31	32	33	34	✗	36	37	38	39	40

WE PAY ON COMPUTER ISSUED TICKETS - TICKETS WITH ERRORS NOT CORRECTED BEFORE START OF GAME WILL BE ACCEPTED AS ISSUED

41	42	43	44	45	46	47	48	49	50
51	52	53	54	55	56	✗	58	59	60
61	62	63	64	65	✗	67	68	69	70
71	72	73	74	✗	76	77	78	79	80

WE ARE NOT RESPONSIBLE FOR KENO RUNNERS TICKETS NOT VALIDATED BEFORE START OF NEXT GAME

$1.00 PER WAY

A Big Board Keno ticket marked with six numbers straight up, a way ticket marked as 2/3 and 1/6 for two groups of three and one group of six, and a King-8 way ticket.

KENO

MARK NUMBER OF SPOTS OR WAYS PLAYED

28/6   8/7   1/8

NO. OF GAMES   TOTAL PRICE
1   $37.00

WINNING TICKETS MUST BE COLLECTED IMMEDIATELY AFTER EACH KENO GAME IS CALLED

1	2	3	4	5	6	7	8	9	10
11	12	13	14	15	16	17	18	19	20
21	22	23	24	25	26	27	28	29	30
31	32	33	34	35	36	37	38	39	40

$1.00 PER WAY

WE PAY ON COMPUTER ISSUED TICKETS - TICKETS WITH ERRORS NOT CORRECTED BEFORE START OF GAME WILL BE ACCEPTED AS ISSUED

41	42	43	44	45	46	47	48	49	50
51	52	53	54	55	56	57	58	59	60
61	62	63	64	65	66	67	68	69	70
71	72	73	74	75	76	77	78	79	80

WE ARE NOT RESPONSIBLE FOR KENO RUNNERS TICKETS NOT VALIDATED BEFORE START OF NEXT GAME

Kings," is a ticket where you mark 8 individual numbers, as in a regular ticket, but you place a small circle over each of your selected numbers.

This makes each number a king, meaning it is to be included in combination with any of the other numbers you picked. The possibilities for this ticket are as follows: 56/6, 28/6, 8/7, and 1/8. At the half-dollar per way rate, this ticket costs $46.50, and if you hit at least three numbers you will be paid as follows:

Hit 3 numbers	pays $	10.00
Hit 4 numbers	pays $	77.00
Hit 5 numbers	pays $	633.50
Hit 6 numbers	pays $	3,660.50
Hit 7 numbers	pays $17,026.50
Hit 8 numbers	pays $69,000.00

Another popular way ticket is a ¹⁹%, which can be played for ten cents per way, a total cost of $19.00 per game. This ticket allows you to mark *all* 80 numbers, generally in vertical groups of four, or as groups of four in squares. The most popular way to play this ticket is to divide the entire 80 numbers into vertical groups of four numbers each. This is very simple to do just by drawing several lines vertically and one line horizontally across the middle of the ticket. The Keno writers can show you how to do it.

On this ticket there are 190 ways to make an 8-spot. You need at least 5 numbers, within your groups, to win anything, but since you are playing *all* the 80 numbers, the 20 numbers drawn in each game often align for a combination of 6, 7, and even 8, all winners for you. For a ten-cent per way bet, you can win $2,000 if you hit *any* 8 numbers, within at least two of your groups, four in each group. In addition, *any* other numbers appearing in *any* of your other groups of four add to your wins and multiply them. It is therefore possible to win several bets at once. If your groups hit, say, four numbers out of four on one, four out of four on another, and three out of four on yet another, you will be paid the one 8-spot winner, *plus* two 7-out-of-8 winners, all combined, as well as all other combinations of 5-and-6-out-of-8.

Yet another popular bet is the Quick Pick, but this is available only in casinos offering computerized Quick Pick Keno. A Quick Pick is a bet where you *do not* mark any numbers on the ticket, merely *how many* numbers you wish to play. You mark, for example, ⅙ on the side or top of the ticket, but no numbers on the inside. Instead you mark the inside of the ticket with the initials QP, and when you hand this ticket to the Keno writer he or she will have the computer pick the numbers for you. If it is offered by the casino you are in, a Quick Pick can be played for any ticket, including any way ticket.

◆| SPECIAL ONE-BET TICKETS |◆

Some casinos offer special one-bet tickets as incentives to get more players to bet more money, by advertising an enormous Keno jackpot. As in real lotteries, winning such a jackpot requires a huge amount of sheer luck. Most of the time it is really better to avoid these tickets because they are more of a marketing ploy than a good bet for the player. The notable exceptions are the Winner Take All (WTA) tickets, and the Last Chance Dance ticket. Winner Take All tickets are one-bet-one-pay tickets, the name of which says it all: the winner takes everything.

In regular Keno if you play, say, a 6-spot ticket, you get paid for hitting three, four, and five out of six numbers, in addition to the jackpot for 6-out-of-6. If, however, you were to play the 6-spot as a Winner Take All ticket, you would *only* be paid if you caught *all* six numbers. No other pays are paid. The cost of these tickets is much higher than the cost of a regular ticket. Minimum bets start at $5, but players can often bet as high as $100. Although casinos often do offer WTA tickets as 6-spots, 5-spots, 4-spots and, in some casinos, 3-spots, the only ones worth the player's while are the 3- and 4-spot WTA tickets. The possibility of hitting the solid 5 or solid 6 numbers out of the 20 numbers drawn is just too slim to gamble this much money on.

Hitting 3 or 4 numbers, on the other hand, is not quite so tough, and in WTA games even a 3- or 4-spot ticket offers some sizable winnings. On regular Keno, for instance, a $5 bet on a 4-spot will pay only $575; but on the 4-spot WTA it pays almost double. The fact that you *do not* get any pays for hitting two or three out of the four numbers on the WTA 4-spot ticket is far outweighed by the $1,100 you get when you hit all four. This does not mean that you will hit a 3-out-of-3 or a 4-out-of-4 winner more often than in betting the same ticket on the regular game, but it does mean that you will get considerably more money for your win when you do hit it.

Another ticket worth mentioning is the 20-spot ticket, often called the "Last Chance Dance" ticket. Again the minimum bet is usually $5, but this ticket also pays a jackpot if you don't hit any of the 20 numbers you picked. In most casinos if you don't hit any numbers on this 20-spot ticket, you will be paid $1,000, though some casinos only offer $500. If you plan to play this ticket, play it in a casino that offers the $1,000 prize. The odds of *not* hitting on this ticket are the same in all Keno games, so why play it in a casino that offers less in prize money? This ticket also offers small payoffs if you hit 1 or 2 numbers, pays nothing if you hit 3, 4, 5, and 6 numbers, pays even money for hitting 7, double your money for hitting 8, and then larger payoffs all the way up to hitting all 20.

Hitting all 20 numbers is nearly impossible, and you will often see that the top jackpot starts at hitting 16 out of 20. In most casinos this top jackpot is upward of $300,000 and can get up to $1 million. So if you hit at least 16 out of 20, you're in the money big time. But the best reason to play this ticket is for the "no hit" payoff. Since there are 80 total numbers available, the odds of you *not* hitting any of the 20 drawn are much better than hitting 16, 17, 18, 19 or all 20 out of the 20 numbers drawn. This is quite a popular ticket and I myself have won the none-out-of-20 prize several times, although I've never hit more than 13 out of 20. This will give you some indication of how difficult it is to hit any jackpots when you play many more than 10 numbers straight up.

One hint: If you play this ticket, group your numbers in remote areas of the Keno ticket. For example, six numbers in the top left-hand corner, six numbers in the top right-hand corner, four in the middle of the ticket on the left side, and four in the middle of the ticket on the right side. This will give you a total of the 20 numbers, but will leave large areas of the Keno ticket open. I've noticed that Keno numbers often run in groups. So if they group where you picked them, you have won one of the jackpots; and if they group in the larger area you left uncovered, then you win the none-out-of-20 payoff.

◆ PROGRESSIVE JACKPOTS AND ◆ LATE NIGHT SPECIALS

Many casinos now offer progressive Keno jackpots, very similar in nature to the progressive jackpots offered on video poker and slots. The principle is the same. The jackpot, as indicated on the progressive meter, grows with each bet made and continues to grow until it is hit. Although such a progressive jackpot, if you hit it, can be very large—often in the hundreds of thousands of dollars—the disadvantage is that you must usually bet at least $5 on a ticket of 8 numbers or more, and have to hit *all the numbers* to win the progressive jackpot. This kind of Keno option is great for advertising, but is in reality nearly impossible to win.

Some casinos also offer Late Night Specials. These are specific Keno betting options made available usually between 1 A.M. and 9 A.M., and are there to attract players during these wee hours when action in the Keno lounge is very slow. One such ticket is a 4-spot where 4-out-of-4 pays $1,000 on a $5 bet, but which, unlike the WTA ticket, also pays $18 for 3-out-of-4. Another such ticket is the 5-spot, which pays $3,600 for 5-out-of-5 on a $5 bet, but also $125 for a 4-out-of-5. Other similar gimmicks are also available, but none really offers the player much advantage relative to, say, standard way tickets.

These tickets are good to play once or twice if you're up that late, and if you hit a winner you will have a better night. Yes, you may be that lucky, but there are smarter ways to bet your Keno dollar.

◆| **SIMPLE STRATEGY** |◆

Since Keno is entirely a game of luck, it would be impossible to offer any bonafide betting strategy. Nevertheless, I can offer a few hints based on many years of observation and play:

1. Keno numbers, as suggested earlier, tend to run in groups more often than not. It is therefore better to group your numbers, rather than mark them all scattered over your Keno ticket.

2. Short-term trends also seem to appear frequently, quite in defiance of any mathematical laws of probability. On such occasions certain numbers will be drawn more often than other numbers. When you first approach the Keno lounge, go to the Keno writer and ask for a printout of the last 10 games. Then look and study the numbers drawn and see if you spot any trends. Also keep this in mind as you play, and bet accordingly.

3. Play "way" tickets rather than straight up tickets. But if you do play a straight up ticket, bet the 6-spot. Or bet the 8-spot as 8 kings on a way ticket, and bet only the 6-spots, 7-spots and the 8-spot. An 8 kings way ticket also allows for 56-5's but, at $1 per way, betting all available options will cost you a great deal of money. My suggestion of playing only the 6's, 7's and the 8 minimizes the expense and maximizes the payoff. By playing like this, if you hit any four numbers, you will be paid for hitting 4-in-6 *plus* 4-in-7 *plus* 4-in-8. Most of the time even small hits like this will either pay for the ticket and give you a free play next game, or, at the very least, give you enough of a return so that the next game costs you even less

in cash outlay. And, if you do hit six numbers or
more, you'll be in the big money.

4. Another great way to bet Keno is to combine a way
   ticket with a 6-spot straight up ticket, or several such
   tickets in combination with each other. This will
   give you more chances for more frequent winners.

5. When playing the Winner Take All tickets, play the
   3-spot or 4-spot tickets only.

6. Never play any ticket where you must pick more
   than 10 numbers, unless it's a way ticket.

7. Frequency is your friend. Play the same numbers as
   many games in a row as you can. Your best bet for
   any straight up ticket is to play the "play and stray"
   option, by buying at least 21 consecutive games.
   This way you don't have to sit in the Keno lounge
   and wait for the games to be played. You can go and
   play something else, or go to dinner, to sleep, even
   back home, and still have up to a year to collect
   any winnings.

8. You can also "wheel" your numbers, meaning you select several numbers as your constant core, and then
   add numbers to them on other tickets in several
   combinations, always keeping your core numbers
   the same on each ticket. This way, if your core numbers hit, your chances of combining them with several of the other numbers are better, and your wins
   are multiplied by each winning ticket. This also
   works for way tickets, if you play more than one.

9. Unless you are playing more than 21 consecutive
   games on the same ticket, *never* forget to claim your
   prize at the conclusion of the last game of your
   ticket sequence.

The attraction of Keno is that the wins are big when
you hit all your numbers. The bad news is the truly bad

odds. In Keno, the house retainer percentage is upward of 28 percent, making Keno by far the worst game, oddswise, of any game offered in the casino.

This said, Keno can nonetheless provide a rewarding experience if you play it smart and don't allocate all your money to it. Keno should be treated as a diversion, a sideline to your regular gaming vacation. Playing Keno can be relaxing and fun, but it can also cost you a good deal of money. Still, if you play way tickets wisely, often such tickets will pay for themselves, giving you financial longevity and thus more chances to win big.

One final piece of advice for all Keno games: Keno requires patience. Lots of it. This is not a fast-action game, so don't expect to get excited by the fervor of it. If you play Keno, keep this in mind, and also remember that patience pays. This is true of all gambling games, but particularly so for Keno. If you would like to play Keno, but the prospect of sitting there for several hours bores you to tears, then buy the multirace ticket in excess of 21 games. This way you're in the Keno action even while you look for quick thrills elsewhere in the casino.

10
VIDEO KENO

The game of Video Keno looks the same and plays the same as Big Board Keno. The differences lie in the speed of the game and the payoff schedules. Big Board Keno is mostly a slow game, with one game played on average every five minutes. But each game in Video Keno lasts only about fifteen seconds, which makes it less boring over any designated play period. The frequency also gives you more chances at winners.

Video Keno works on the same principle as other computerized slots. Although there is no handle to pull on a Video Keno machine, or any reels that spin, there is the customary "start" button that you push to begin the game. In addition, the software program that runs the game is very similar to the one that runs the computerized slots, including Video Poker. Basically, the only differences are in the graphics—the pictures that make up winning combinations. In Video Poker these graphics are playing cards; on reel slots, these may be a variety of pictures; in Video Keno, they are numbers. But the principle by which the program selects the random winning combinations is the same.

Like all slot machines, Video Keno machines pay relative to play. Each certain number of plays the machine will hit certain pays, and the jackpot. With 80 numbers to pick from, it is easy to see that winning combinations may not happen with as great a frequency as in, say, Video Poker. However, this is more than offset by the relative speed of the game, and by the generally much higher jackpots.

In Big Board Keno the minimum bet is usually $1 or $2, but Video Keno is offered in a variety of denominations, from nickels to dollars. Most Video Keno machines are the 25-cent kind, and will take from one to four quarters per bet.

◆ | HOW TO RECOGNIZE VIDEO KENO | ◆

There are two styles of Video Keno machines, both easily identifiable. Most machines are very tall, dark red in color, and have two video display screens. There are also slant-top Video Keno machines, but they are not as common. Most casinos, and players, prefer the tall version of the machine.

To the left side of the machine, and connected to the machine by a cord, is a device that looks somewhat like a pen. This is the so-called "magic wand" that you will use to select your numbers prior to the start of the game.

On Video Keno machines, the top screen shows the payoff schedules and the bottom screen, the one at eye level, shows the same 80-number display that you find on the main board in Big Board Keno. The payoff schedules displayed on the top screen change according to the number of spots you mark and the number of coins you play.

Video Keno machines are about twice the size of regular slot machines, and each has a yellow sign on the top

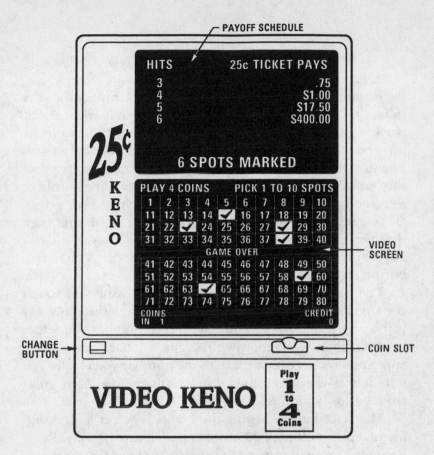

A Video Keno machine.

identifying it as Keno. This makes them very prominent in any area of the casino. Many casinos have hundreds of them, while other casinos have only a few. Because of the look of these machines, and the multitude of betting options they offer, many casual visitors find them intimidating and confusing. In truth, however, these machines can offer just about the best payout-to-investment ratio of any gambling game. And they are extremely easy to play.

◆│ HOW TO PLAY VIDEO KENO │◆

Although a Keno slot machine can *look* confusing, it is in fact just like the Keno played in the Keno lounge, and it works exactly the same way. There are 80 numbers on the screen, and you can pick from one to ten numbers at a time. The first thing you do after depositing your coin(s) is press the "erase" button. In so doing you wipe out all the numbers selected by the player who played the machine before you. Of course, if you wish to play exactly the same numbers that were already selected by the previous player, all you have to do is deposit your coins and then press the start button instead of the erase button.

The next step is to pick up the magic wand and touch the tip of it to the video screen directly over the numbers you wish to select, one by one. With each number you select the machine will sound a chime and a "check" mark will appear on the screen in place of the number you chose. Ten numbers is the maximum that existing Video Keno machines allow you to select.

The start button begins the game. When it is pressed, the machine will pick 20 numbers, and, as with Big Board Keno, the more numbers that match the ones you selected, the more you win. The Video Keno screen is generally blue in color, and as the machine picks the winning numbers for that particular game, the winning numbers light up on the screen in red. If the winning number selected is among the numbers you chose, then a red "tick" mark will appear over that selected number, indicating this is a winning number, and a chime will often sound. This process is repeated for all the numbers so picked by the machine.

A Video Keno machine is a computer, much like Video Poker, and the computer program that randomly selects the Keno numbers to be drawn during any one game is very similar to the program that runs the Video Poker games. Of course, a Video Keno machine has many more options, since there are eighty numbers total from which the computer program randomly selects only twenty. It is, therefore, not as easy to pick winning combinations as often as, say, on a 9/6 video poker machine, but then the payoffs are also considerably bigger for several of the top jackpots; also, the investment necessary can be smaller, because you need only play one coin to start the game and still have a chance at the top payoff, while in Video Poker it will take a five-coin bet to do the same.

Most people play 6-spots, and the payoffs are quite remarkable. Although there is no payoff for zero, one or two numbers out of six, for a 25-cent bet Video Keno machines will pay seventy-five cents for 3-out-of-6, $1 for 4, $17.50 for 5, and $400.00 for the full 6. This is a very high payoff relative to the investment. The fact that you can get a high payoff like this, relative to the amount at risk, makes Video Keno a good bet. These pays are doubled for the next coin played. So, if you play fifty cents, your 6-out-of-6 jackpot is $800 instead of $400. A bet of seventy-five cents will pay $1,200, and a bet of four quarters will pay $1,600. Actually, in some casinos the seventy-five cent bet will pay $1,199.75 instead of the $1,200. This is done to keep the jackpot under $1,200, which, as I will discuss shortly, must be reported at once to the IRS. Keeping the jackpot below this tax limit can save you and the casino a lot of paperwork and hassles.

Granted, it is not easy to hit all six numbers, but then no slot play is an easy proposition. But unlike other slots where for four quarters you may win, say, 1,600 *quarters*, on Video Keno you win 1,600 *dollars*. A big difference.

There are a few other reasons that 6-spots are the favorite among players of Video Keno. One is that the machine pays 3:1 for hitting 3-out-of-6. This is a very good payoff, which occurs quite frequently and provides you with a good return even when you don't hit the top jackpot. Another reason is that on a 6-spot there are *four* ways out of seven possible which provide you with a win, and only three ways in which there is no win. Of course, there are plenty of bets other than 6-spots in Video Keno. But although you can pick up to 10-spots, generally the fewer spots you pick the better your chances of a win. To be sure, this can get quite ridiculous. Often I see people play 1-, 2-, and 3-spots, spend a good deal of their money, and even when they hit their numbers, wind up not even recouping their investment. As a general rule, your best bets are the 6-, 7-, and 8-spots.

The 6-spot is the best option because it offers the most chances for a payoff. Picking six out of the 20 numbers drawn by the Video Keno machine is easier than picking, say, 10. Of all the years I have been playing Video Keno I have seen 10-out-of-10 hit only once. In playing the 6-spot, most of the time you will receive pays up to 5-out-of-6, but the solid 6 will hit more often than any other number combination available in Video Keno.

The 7-spot usually provides the best chance for hitting 6-out-of-7, which pays $100.00 for a twenty-five cent bet. A solid 7 is just as rare as any solid hit, other than a solid 6-spot, but does happen more frequently than the solid 8. The 8-spot is good to play because a lot of the time you can expect to hit the 6-out-of-8 for $24.75, giving you more money to play with. As I have pointed out throughout this book, playing with casino money is better than playing with your own. However, you should not expect to hit the solid 8. This is very rare. Most of the time you should look for the 7-out-of-8, which will pay you $413.50 for a twenty-five cent bet. This occurs about as often as a solid 6, but the advantage of playing the 8-spot is that you still do have a chance of hitting the solid 8; by playing the 6-spot you only have a chance for a solid 6. Nonetheless, as far as strategy advice goes, the 6-spot is still the best option.

Playing a 5-spot is fun if all you're after is a small jack-pot or just want to pass some time. Otherwise it provides little opportunity for some decent dollars. Same goes for the 4-spot, which is best employed if you wish to win some casino money first before playing for the bigger jackpots. But be careful not to blow your whole bankroll chasing a 4-spot. Most of the time if the machine you are playing hits the 4-spot, it would have hit a 6, 7, or even 8, so normally you are better off starting with the bigger jackpot combinations and sticking to them.

◆| SIMPLE STRATEGY |◆

Like Big Board Keno, Video Keno is a game of pure luck. Still, many of the same hints for smart play in Big Board Keno also apply here. But because Video Keno also shares many characteristics with other slot machines, some of those hints will also apply. I therefore offer, in addition, a few suggestions specific to the peculiarities of Video Keno:

1. Group your numbers. Video Keno machines, as with Big Board Keno, have a tendency to group numbers. This is a quirk of the machine's program, but you can exploit it to your advantage. For example, the numbers 25, 26, 27, 35, 36, and 37, seem to hit more frequently than others. This is a favorite 6-spot among regular Video Keno players.

2. Play a 6-spot more than any other combination. It has the best investment-to-payoff ratio in Video Keno. The 6-spot is a better bet than other combinations in Video Keno because it offers the most frequent hits, and it will generally allow you more playing time and cost you less to play.

3. Changing your numbers is Keno suicide. Whatever numbers you pick, stick to them for the duration of your play. Even if the numbers are not hitting, eventually they will. The more they are *not* hitting, the better chance you have that they will all come in.

4. While in slot play it is always advisable to play the maximum number of coins, in Video Keno the advantage lies in exactly the opposite. Video Keno machines offer many big pays even when betting the minimum one-coin requirement. Play twenty-five cents per bet until you win. Then double your bet. If you win again, add another quarter and play for seventy-five cents per bet, and if you win again, up this to the maximum coins of $1.

5. Choose a machine to play, and play it as you would any slot machine: with discipline. Select one that has not hit the jackpot recently or one that has not hit a jackpot on a certain combination of numbers.

   For example, a machine may have hit a jackpot on a 6-spot, but it may still hit a jackpot on a 7-spot, or the 8-spot. Also, don't chase your money. If your machine is not paying, don't stick more of your money into it. A $20 stake—playing twenty-five cents at a time—is a good gauge by which to determine whether this machine will pay. If it doesn't, move to another or quit for this session. (You might even want to reread the pointers I gave in the chapter on slot machines.)

6. Select your bankroll for Video Keno play before you begin. Then buy all the change for your entire bankroll and·put it all in the machine, coin by coin, one for each game. The machine employs a "credits" display, like most slot machines. All winning pays will run up on this credit meter. If, after you have played all your starting bankroll for this session (your ses-

sion stake), the winnings shown on your credit meter are close to even with your starting bankroll, or greater than the amount of your starting bankroll, your machine is playing well and will likely hit you a jackpot. Continue to play it to either half your session stake, or twice your money—or, of course, the top jackpot.

Although it is a good alternative to fast action in the casino, oddswise Video Keno, like Big Board Keno, is not the best game to play. Its attractiveness lies in the large pays it can provide when the total numbers you picked, in any group, all hit. But Video Keno also requires a lot of patience. It can be a very frustrating game, and quite time-consuming. If you have no time and no patience, don't play it. But if you wish to relax, gamble with little to win a lot, and you have the time to enjoy the casino and free cocktails, settle yourself down in front of a Video Keno machine for a few hours and you're likely to walk away with a sizable win.

11
TAXES AND SLOTS

At this point I feel it is important to mention Uncle Sam. Most players do not realize how long the government's arm is when it comes to collecting taxes. In gaming, any slot machine or Video Poker winnings over $1,200, or any Big Board Keno jackpot winnings over $1,500, are subject to federal tax, and to state tax in some states. Therefore if you hit a jackpot over $1,200, be prepared to pay up. As far as the IRS is concerned, this is reportable income. In fact, the letter of the law requires that *any* wins be reported as income, even though such wins may be under the limit mandating an official report. This can get truly ridiculous because to totally comply, even a win of twenty-five cents would need to be so reported as income.

If you do hit a jackpot that requires a mandatory tax report, the casino floorman will ask you for identification and your Social Security number, then take it to the casino cage, verify it, write up a tax slip, and ask you to sign it.

If you refuse, you won't be paid the jackpot. Casinos are required by law to report such jackpot wins to the IRS. This basically means that your gaming dollar is taxed twice: once when you earn it as part of your paycheck, and the second time when you win it back after first losing it in the machine. It's not fair, and I hope casinos will succeed in getting Uncle Sam to stop double-dipping.

This form of taxation does not apply to table game wins, although the IRS has been trying for a long time to find ways of taxing such wins. The problem for the IRS has been in identifying what specifically constitutes a table win. When a player goes to the casino cage to cash in gaming chips, who's to say whether these gaming chips were "won," or if they are merely the chips the player "bought" prior to playing and then did not lose? It is fortunate that this gray area exists. There are already enough taxes levied on casinos and casino wins, and on players. Should the IRS succeed in such taxation practices it would instantly kill the gaming industry.

But when you win on a slot machine, or in Keno, the amount of your win in excess of the taxable limits is clearly visible and therefore easily identified. Consequently, it is a good idea to keep track of your gaming *losses*. If you are ever audited, such losses can be used as tax deductions against reported gaming wins.

One more thing. If you are not a U.S. citizen or legal resident, the taxes will be withheld by the casino before you are paid. Uncle Sam wants to make sure he gets his cut.

Glossary of Gambling Terms

The words used to describe gambling games and the way they are played are often as interesting as the games themselves. Some very colorful words have been created over the years which apply specifically to gaming. As an added means of assisting you in your gaming success, I have compiled a short list of some of the most widely used gambling terms.

Ace   The highest card in each of the four suits in a standard deck of 52 cards. In Blackjack, can count as 1 or 11. In Craps, the single spot on the dice.

Ace-Deuce   In Craps, the two-dice combination of 1 and 2.

Action   The amount of money you bet; the total amount of money wagered in any casino game during any given shift.

Ahead   Winning during any particular session of play.

All Across   In Craps, referring to a bet that covers all the box numbers. Also known as "across the board."

All In   In Poker, having no more money left on the table to continue betting on any given hand—often results in a side pot for other players still betting beyond your last bet; also means "broke."

Ante   In Poker, a mandatory bet required from all players in most poker games as a means of paying to be in the next hand.

Backboard   In Craps, the side of the table farthest away from the current shooter, against which the dice are thrown.

Back Line   In Craps, the "don't pass" and the "don't come" areas on the table layout.

Back-to-Back   In Poker, referring to two cards of the same number or face value; means the same as "wired."

Bank   The House money in any given game.

Banker   The individual who covers all the action in any given game over a specific period of time. This is usually the House, but can, in some games, also be a player.

Best Bet   A bet in which the odds are better for the player than they are for the House, or at least substantially diminish the House edge in any particular game.

Bet   Any wager placed by players in any gambling game.

Bet the Limit   To wager the most money allowed by the casino on any given table in any game.

Bird Cage   The machine that draws Keno numbers by rolling them out one at a time; similar to "the bubble," which is a different apparatus for drawing Keno numbers by blowing them out with forced air (both apply to Big Board Keno).

Black   In Roulette, a bet on all of the 18 numbers colored in black, as opposed to red.

Blackjack   In Blackjack, a natural 21.

Blind Bet   In Poker, a bet players make before receiving their cards or before looking at their cards.

Bluff   In Poker, to bet aggressively despite holding a bad hand in an attempt to make the other players think you have better cards than you do.

Box Cars   In Craps, the two-dice combination of 6 and 6.

Boxman   A casino employee who runs the Craps game.

Box Numbers   In Craps, the numbers 4,5,6,8,9, and 10. Also known as "place numbers."

Breaking Hand   In Blackjack, any two-card hand that can exceed 21 with just one more card drawn.

Burn a Card   To remove from play one or more cards from the top of the deck immediately after a shuffle and prior to the start of a new game.

Bust   In Blackjack, to go over 21; to go broke.

Buy Bet   In Craps, a bet placed at true odds for which the player pays a 5 percent commission at the time of making the bet. This is the same as "buying a number," and can be made for or against any point number.

Cage   An area of the casino where all the money is kept and chips stored. Mostly know as "casino cage," but "cage" for short. Here you cash your chips for cash, but you can also get credit, cash your checks, draw and pay off markers, get credit card cash advances, and transact any other monetary business with the casino.

Call   In Poker, betting the same amount, in turn, as was bet before you by other players; signifies you are still in the game but do not wish to raise the bets. On the last hand, if you do not wish to raise the bets, this also means the same as "see."

Card Counter   In Blackjack, a person who keeps mental track of the value of cards drawn in order to better calculate what cards he might draw and then bets accordingly.

Cash In   To exchange gaming chips for cash, done at the cage.

Catch A Number   In Keno, to select any winning number.

Check In Poker, to stay in a specific round of any hand without making a bet—this can be done only if no other player has made a bet. Also means a "casino marker," which is just like a check from your checkbook.

Column Bet In Roulette, a bet on twelve numbers lined up in a column on the table layout.

Come Bet In Craps, a bet in the "come" area on the layout, made after the shooter has established his point.

Come Out In Craps, the first roll of dice by a new shooter, or by the same shooter after he or she has made the previous point.

Cover To back all bets as Banker in any given game over a given period of time. In Poker, to bet the same cumulative amount as the players just before you in turn—same as "call."

Craps In Craps, the numbers 2, 3, and 12.

Crap Out In Craps, to throw any craps on the come out roll. Also means to lose on the point by rolling a 7 before making the established point.

Croupier In Roulette, the French name for a dealer.

Cut To divide a deck of cards into two piles prior to dealing. Mostly done by players. The two piles are then reassembled with the top pile going to the bottom of the deck, always done by the dealer.

Dead Card A card that is taken out of play because it has been exposed inadvertently by the dealer or one of the players and seen by other players. If the card is exposed by a player, but not seen by other players, it can remain in play at the request of the player who so exposed it. Any card exposed by the dealer is automatically a dead card, which often results in a dead hand. This dealer error is often called a "misdeal."

Dead Hand In any card game a hand that is canceled and begun anew following a mistake by the dealer or one of the players. Most common in Poker, but not unusual in Blackjack.

Deal The distribution of cards to players to begin a hand.

Dealer The man or woman who distributes all cards to players over the course of a given hand.

Deuce Shorthand name for the number 2 in any game.

Don't Come In Craps, a bet made after the point is established, placed in the "don't come" area of the layout. This is the exact opposite of the "come" bet.

Don't Pass In Craps, a bet against the shooter, meaning that player is betting that the shooter will not make his point before rolling 7. Also known as "wrong way" or "back line," this is the exact opposite of the "pass line" bet.

Double Down In Blackjack, to double your bet on the first two cards dealt to you. This can usually be done on any first two cards dealt, but some casinos only allow this on first two card combinations of 10 and 11.

Down Card Any card dealt face down. In Blackjack, the first card the dealer receives.

Draw To receive a card from the dealer after the initial set of cards in a hand have been dealt.

Drop Box A secure box under the gaming table into which the dealer, via a cash chute, stuffs all the money he receives when players buy gaming chips.

Easy In Craps, referring to a roll of the dice in which the two-dice combinations of 4, 6, 8, or 10 are rolled in ways other than pairs.

Even Money A winning bet payoff equal to the original amount wagered.

Exposed Card   Any card in a hand of cards dealt face up.

Face Card   Any king, queen or jack in a deck of cards.

Field   In Craps, the numbers 2, 3, 4, 9, 10, 11, and 12, marked in a special area on the table layout called "field."

Field Bet   In Craps, a bet on the "field" numbers.

Fifth Street   In Poker, the fifth round of betting.

Fishing   In Poker, overplaying a bad hand up through the last card dealt in the hope of catching the one card that makes your bad hand into a winner.

First Base   In Blackjack, the first position at the table to the left of the dealer. The player in that position will always receive the first cards dealt in the game.

Five Card Draw   The simplest and most straightforward variety of Poker on which almost all Video Poker games are based.

Flat Bet   Any bet that pays off at even money.

Flush   In Poker, a hand with any five cards of the same suit.

Fold   In Poker, to throw your cards in and drop out of a hand.

Four of a Kind   In Video Poker and Poker, any four cards of the same, or any four of the same face card—e.g., four 6's, four kings, etc.

Front Line   In Craps, a bet on the pass line or come.

Full House   In Video Poker and Poker, a hand containing any three of a kind combined with another pair.

Hand   A player's own set of cards at any given point in the game; also used to describe the round of cards in any given card game.

Hardways   In Craps, a roll of the dice in which the two-dice combination totals of 4, 6, 8, or 10 are rolled in pairs: 2 + 2, 3 + 3, 4 + 4, and 5 + 5.

High-Low   In Craps, a one-roll bet that either a 2 or a 12 will be rolled. Each combination can be thrown only one way.

High Roller   Any gambler who bets a lot of money.

Hit   In Blackjack, to ask for another card after the first two cards have been dealt. This can be done either by saying, "hit me," or by a movement of the hand, or by scratching your cards on the table layout.

Hole Card   Same as down card.

House   Any casino where gambling games are offered, and where the casino also banks the games.

House Limit   The most the House will allow you to bet on any single hand or on any game they provide.

House Numbers   In Roulette, the 0 and 00 on the wheel and corresponding table layout.

House Percentage   The percentage of all money bet on any particular game that, by virtue of the rules of that game, the House takes in as income. Same as "House edge" and "House advantage."

Insurance   In Blackjack, a bet made to protect your hand against a dealer's possible natural 21—dealer's blackjack. Normally done when the dealer's up card is an ace. If you also hold a blackjack, instead of betting insurance you can also ask for "even money."

In the Hole   Losing during any particular gambling session.

Jackpot   The top prize on a slot machine, Video Poker machine, and any progressive table and Keno game.

Joker   The fifty-third card in a standard deck of cards, mostly used as a wild card.

Keno   A numbers game similar to a lottery.

Keno Board   The big illuminated panel on which numbers drawn during a game of Keno are displayed.

Layout   The design printed on the felt table covering on any given table game showing where, and on what, players can make their bets.

Let It Ride   After winning on a given hand, roll, or spin, to leave your original bet *plus* all your winnings on the table as a bet for the next hand, roll, or spin. Also known as "pressing" the bet.

Line Bet   In Craps, a bet on the pass line. In Roulette, a bet on six numbers displayed on the table layout in two columns of three side by side.

Lucky Loser   In Blackjack, a hand with good value that loses to a one-better by the dealer. Can apply to any game where this occurs.

Lucky Stiff   In Blackjack, any two-card hand totaling between 12 and 16 that is turned into a winning hand by a lucky draw of one or more cards.

Marker   Casino check issued to a player who has established credit; a nondenominational chip used to identify a certain position or value; in Roulette, small marker chips are used to identify the value of gaming chips in play; also the crayon used to mark Keno numbers.

Martingale   A silly betting progression system in gambling that calls for a player to double his bets after each loss in the expectation that eventually the player will win and therefore recoup all his losses, plus win the amount of his original bet. Good in theory but impossible in practice because House table limits are designed to prevent the possibility of such infinite progression betting systems.

Misdeal   A dealer's card-handling error which renders the hand null.

Money Plays   A betting option offered at some table games that permit the wagering of cash as well as gaming chips.

Natural   In Blackjack, a 21 on the first two cards. In Craps, a 7 on the come out roll. In Baccarat, a two-card total of 8 or 9.

No Dice   In Craps, an invalid throw of the dice, usually called by the Boxman or Stickman when the dice are thrown, or bounce, over the side of the table.

Odds   The mathematical likelihood that a certain event will or will not occur. In Craps, an extra bet in addition to the original bet.

Odds On   In Craps, requesting to have odds on come bets in action on the come out roll.

Off   In Craps, referring to any bet which the player has temporarily suspended.

One Roll Bet   In Craps, any bet which wins or loses on a single roll of the dice.

Pair   In any game, two of the same; e.g., in card games and Video Poker two kings, two aces, two nines, etc.; in Craps, hard ways, box cars and aces; in slots, two cherries, two sevens, etc.

Parlay   To repeatedly bet one's cumulative winnings on the subsequent event, or in a series of successive bets in one or more games. Mostly used in sport betting using a bet called the parlay card.

Pass   In Poker, to signal no bet but stay in the hand. This can only be done if no player before you in turn has made a bet and is the same as "check." In Craps, a win on the pass line.

Pass Line   In Craps, an area marked on the table layout and referred to as the front line; bets on the pass line are also known as "right way" bets. The exact opposite of "don't pass."

Pat   Referring to any hand of cards on which the player declines to take a hit or draw.

Payline   A line on the window display of a slot machine along which the reel symbols that determine a winner must line up.

Payoff   The return on a winning wager.

Payoff Odds   The odds at which winning bets are paid off.

Percentage   The amount of your bet the House keeps by paying you at less than true odds when you win.

Picture Card   Any king, queen, or jack in a deck of cards. Same as face card.

Pit   An area in the casino around which a collection of table games is arranged. Off limits to all but casino personnel.

Pit Boss   The man or woman who supervises all games arranged around the pit.

Place Bet   In Craps, a bet on any of the numbers 4, 5, 6, 8, 9, or 10.

Point   In Craps, the numbers 4, 5, 6, 8, 9, and 10, when any one of them is rolled immediately following the come out roll.

Pot   In Poker, the sum of all bets laid on a given hand, to be awarded to the player with the winning hand.

Press a Bet   To increase the size of a bet. Often done after a win by the amount of that win.

Proposition Bet   In Craps, any bet other than pass, don't pass, come, and don't come.

Puck   A disk the size of a hockey puck, white on one side and black on the other, used to indicate the point in Craps. A thinner version, with the word "dealer" on it, is used to identify the player who will receive the last cards in the first round of Texas Hold-Em Poker.

Push   In Blackjack, a tied hand—no win and no loss. Applies also to any other bet in any game where no loss and no win occurs.

Rack   A storage device to hold gaming chips or slot tokens.

Rail   In Craps, the two sets of grooves at the top of the table, used by players to store their gaming chips while playing.

Raise   In Poker, to increase the amount of the previous bet.

Rake   In Poker, the amount of money, by percentage, that the House progressively deducts from the pot during each hand.

Red   In Roulette, a bet on all the eighteen numbers colored in red, as opposed to black.

See   In Poker, to call a bet in the last round and after the last raise.

Royal Flush   In Poker and Video Poker, a hand containing a 10, jack, queen, king, and ace, all of the same suit, in any order.

Seven Card Stud   The Poker game where seven cards are dealt to each player, first two face down, next four face up, finally one card face down.

Seven Out   In Craps, to roll a 7 after the point has been established, thereby ending the game and the shooter's turn with the dice.

Shill　A casino employee who plays a given table game with house money in order either to give the impression of activity, or to fill up a short-handed game.

Shoe　A shoebox-shaped plastic box designed to hold several decks of cards, intended to make dealing easier in games using more than two decks of cards.

Shooter　In Craps, the person rolling the dice at any given time.

Shuffle　To mix up the cards before the start of the next series of hands.

Six and Over　In Blackjack, a hand of six or more cards totaling 21 or less. In some casinos an automatic win, often paying 2:1.

Sixth Street　In Poker, the sixth round of betting.

Snake Eyes　In Craps, the two-dice combination of 1 and 1.

Soft Hand　In Blackjack, any two-card combination of an ace and any card other than a 10-value or face card. So called because the ace can count as either 1 or 11.

Split　In Blackjack, to divide any first two cards of the same value into separate hands.

Split Bet　In Roulette, a bet on two numbers made by placing a chip on the line between those two numbers on the table layout.

Stake　The amount of money you allocate to any gambling session.

Stand　In Blackjack, to decline to take any more cards. Also known as "staying pat." Can apply to any game where this decision is up to the player.

Stick　In Craps, the long hooked wand used to move the dice around the table.

Stickman In Craps, the man or woman who wields the stick.

Stiff In Blackjack, any two-card hand totaling 12 through 16.

Straight In Poker and Video Poker, a hand of five cards of consecutive value, such as 7, 8, 9, 10, jack.

Straight Flush In Poker and Video Poker, a hand of five cards of consecutive value, all of the same suit.

Straight Royal Flush In Video Poker, on specific machines so identified, a hand of five cards constituting a royal flush lined up in sequence: either 10-J-Q-K-A, or A-K-Q-J-10. This is also known in some casinos as a "Reversible Royal Flush."

Sucker Bet Any bet in which the casino's in-built advantage is so heavily stacked against the player that getting a win is almost impossible. Also, any bet which is offered on any game with bad odds, but which can also be made differently in the same game with more favorable odds, such as Big 6 and Big 8 in Craps.

Third Base In Blackjack, the last position on the table and therefore the last to receive a card before the dealer.

Three of a Kind In Poker and Video Poker, any three of the same number value, or any three face cards which are the same—e.g., three kings.

Toke A tip for the dealer, or any casino employee.

Up Card Any card dealt face up. In Blackjack, the second card a dealer deals himself.

Vigorish The commission paid by players to the House, per the rules of a given game. Known as "vig" for short.

Working In Craps, referring to any players' bets which that player had called "off" but now wants back in action.

Special Thanks

In addition to the great people I mentioned at the beginning of this book, I would also like to express my gratitude and appreciation to a few more special friends.

My dear friend Larry Levit, who has stuck it out with me through good times and bad. Larry has been the one constant in my life whose faith in me has never faltered.

Dr. Davis McCaughey, former governor of the State of Victoria, Australia, and Master of Ormond College, University of Melbourne, and Professor Lauchlan Chipman, my mentor at the University of Melbourne and the University of Wollongong, Australia.

Roger Gross, editor of *Casino Player* Magazine, who published my first story many years ago; Richard Ballen, a longtime Las Vegas casino executive, whom I first met several years ago at the Las Vegas Hilton, and who has been a solid friend ever since.

Edwin Slogar, a trusted friend who has always been there for me. Eddie is a talented screenwriter and producer with whom I have had the opportunity of working on several motion picture and television projects.

Michael Harrison, my attorney, without whose help and guidance many years ago I could not have done what I am doing now. Esther Morrison, also an attorney, who has provided me with much valuable assistance over many years.

Mr. Phil Cooper, Assistant Vice President of Public Relations and Advertising at Caesars Palace in Las Vegas and all my friends at Caesars Palace.

Barbara Donohue, Kati Smith, Steve Thompson, General Manager of the Fremont Hotel and Casino; Don Payne of the Las Vegas News Bureau; Bobby Berosini and his wife, Joan; Steve Reed of Positive Images Photography Studios in Las Vegas; Debbie Prisbrey from KLAS-TV 8 in Las Vegas; Bruce Boring, Jerry Dominguez, Paulette Theresa, Bill "Vasili" Sousoures, Ricardo Arenciba, Andrew Hooker, Vicki Thomas, Ivan Passer, Milos Forman, Nadine Massey, Ann Robert, Caren Frank, Mark Beaver, Christine Amore, and still more who all know me and how I feel about them.

And a very special personal thanks to Le Roy Neiman. I have spent many days with this remarkable world-renowned artist at his home and studio in New York, at many of his exhibitions, and at the Playboy Mansion in Hollywood. Knowing him has given me focus in my endeavors and provided me with a richness of creative experience I could not have received otherwise.

I also wish to thank Hugh Hefner for the many wonderful times I was privileged to spend at his home.

And finally my two best friends from across the seas, Neil Mummery and his family, and Lilli Michelson and little MRM, both from Melbourne, Australia.

To all these friends, and the many not listed by name but not forgotten, I give my sincere thanks and appreciation for enriching my life.

And to any reader who would like to contact me I offer my address care of *Casino* Magazine:

Casino Magazine
c/o Minnmedia, Inc.
15 South Fifth Street, Suite 900
Minneapolis, MN 55402

I will be glad to answer any gaming questions as part of my regular articles in *Casino* Magazine.

I wish you good fortune, luck, and success at the casino games you play.

Victor H. Royer

Index